Dating 911

The Ultimate Guide to Internet Dating Safety

"I'm quite sure that in the future we'll see some college course on the emerging dynamic of electronic psychology. I know for a fact that every day there are scores of law enforcement officers working in this very area trying to pose as young boys and girls to bait child predators on the Internet. My purpose in writing this book is to give you the same tools that they use—the mindset of a cyber-cop."

Dating 911

The Ultimate Guide to Internet Dating Safety

Chief Dennis Nagy (ret.)

Writers Advantage
New York Lincoln Shanghai

Dating 911
The Ultimate Guide to Internet Dating Safety

Writers Advantage
an imprint of iUniverse, Inc.

For information address:
iUniverse
2021 Pine Lake Road, Suite 100
Lincoln, NE 68512
www.iuniverse.com

ISBN: 0-595-26333-X

Printed in the United States of America

Disclaimer

Although the incidents in "Dating 911" are true, all screen names have been changed.

All first and last names have also been changed.

At no time in this publication have I used an actual screen name of any individual.

No domains or Internet service providers are listed or portrayed in any way to imply that any of them were the service providers that I was using while in e-mail or chat.

At no time has any screen name been associated with or connected in any way with any Internet service.

No incident depicted here is implied in any way to intimate, assume or otherwise relate to a personal incident that I may have encountered with any specific person. Incidents have been dramatized for artistic content.

In all cases occupations, ages and descriptions have been changed to protect the identities of actual people.

Screen names used are purely fictitious and have been made up for artistic endeavor. Any person who may have that screen name or match any description is purely coincidental.

Any person who may have had a similar event in their life or who may have had similar circumstances is purely a chance coincidence.

This book is dedicated to all the single people out there—looking for their own special someone.

Acknowledgments

Dating.911, The Ultimate Guide to Internet Dating Safety was literally a labor of love for me. Since the mere thought of writing the book thru today—I must say that I have grown from a novice to an experienced Internet relationship expert. I would be remiss in not thanking my many "web" friends, "cyber-family" members along with the good ☺ and not so good ☹ Internet dates that made the completion of this book possible.

Support and encouragement was always flowing from many family members and friends. From the bottom of my heart, I would like to sincerely thank David Csimbok, Mark Dobrovolsky, Robin Patric, Debbie Daniels, Debbie Bischoff, Rev. Taras Chubenko, Rick & Jan McGillis, Joe & Tina Sica, Mike & Laura Saccone, and Steve & Anna Tardiff, Alice Catino, Cynthia and Matt Soroka, your words of encouragement and positive thoughts made a dream possible for me.

Extra special thanks goes to my two daughters, Stephanie and Amber and my step-children Ricky and Rachel who contributed to the book in their own special way.

Just like you, my readers, I was on a quest to find a special someone. I must say that I was blessed to find my "Internet Sweetheart" online and she has been alongside me throughout our entire "exciting" journey. Thank you Diane for your endless job of editing and re-editing and for always pushing me to go the step beyond.

Special thanks to the "movers and shakers" at iUniverse. Your professional guidance and direction helped to make this publication possible.

And lastly, thanks to you my readers…I wrote it all for you!

Dennis

PS:
If you have an interesting internet dating story you would like to share, please visit us at our web site: www.Dating-911.com. Dating-911 second edition is in the works and we'd like to use your story.

Happy Dating!

Contents

Dating 911

On September 11th, 2001 the tragedy at the World Trade Center, Washington, and in a field in Pennsylvania impacted not only the political and economic climate in the United States, but also affected the sociology of all American's.

In developing relationships with other people, in business or in friendship, everyone was affected in many ways, on multiple levels. Basic routines were changed as well as the way we viewed every new face that came into sight. As a result, it became increasingly difficult to see the new neighbor from down the street, or who recently moved in next door, through the same eyes. It was no longer possible to automatically trust a smile or simple gesture—suspicion crept into our lives, and unfortunately, establishing new relationships became even more difficult. We all began to think about people we knew and what we knew about them.

I was at home on September 11th, in the process of both writing and book research, when I learned about the tragedy that has become indelible in our minds. The TV was on; it's always on, usually in the background, to keep up on what's going on in the world. As I saw the planes begin to strike, first the towers and then the Pentagon, I immediately got back into action.

I had been retired from the police department for two years, but occasionally helped out in different volunteer capacities. I was involved in local and state emergency management organizations for almost twenty years. Within an hour, I was sitting behind the desk at the County Emergency Management command post helping with staging some of our counties responding volunteers.

During the course of my nearly twenty hours at the command center, I took innumerable telephone calls from just about everyone; people who wanted to help, people who needed help, and many of the very generous responding heroes whom I worked with over the years, willing to risk their lives in the service of others. As the day, and eventually the night, wore on, calls began to come in from family members looking for information about their loved ones.

In the back of my mind, I knew that this was the beginning of a new way that people would think about some of the relationships they had. The fact that people began to appreciate some of their family and friends, became more immediately apparent. The fact that before September 11th they just took for granted that they would be home for dinner, or there to borrow the lawn-mower, soon was replaced by the reality that some of them would never be coming home again.

As the news came in, it became clear that many of the terrorists that were involved had been just everyday people. The same people that you walked past on the street, or shared a seat with on the subway. I knew that everyone in America would begin to feel very differently about the people they saw. There was a growing suspicion of anyone who seemed like a stranger, someone who was different in some small way. I knew that meeting a person, and extending a hand of friendship, would not be the same, ever again.

I finished up my tour of duty at the command center and after sleeping a few restless hours, I called back to see how things were going. By now, more than 30 hours had passed, things began to settle down with response, the recovery process was beginning, and everyone was waiting to see what would happen next.

As the days passed and turned into weeks, and weeks into months, I saw that things were not getting any better. Checking clubs, dating boards, personal ads and other sources that I regularly monitored for my book, I saw a decline in people "looking" for other people. Initially I thought that it was a kind of respect, sort of a "mourning" period for the nation. People were not celebratory throughout the winter holiday season and the spring thaw was no better. By the time summer came, I felt certain that some healing would take place. It wasn't happening. Each day saw a new "terror alert." The news was unrelenting in information about new Al Qaida information. It seemed that if you tried to feel normal, something would happen, somewhere, that changed your mind. We were becoming a very suspicious nation.

We found it hard to ignore the anthrax threat, the suicide bombings, and the threats to the air that we breathe, the water supply we needed, and all of the places that we traditionally went to for solace. Sporting events, theaters, shopping malls, churches and synagogues, mosques and other places of worship, all took on a new name in our growing wartime vernacular; "Targets". Public transportation was dreaded, as it became a magnet for "would be" terrorists.

So how can you meet someone in the post 9-11 world and try to resume a normal and meaningful life with another person? It has changed since September 11th, but it isn't hopeless. Being more careful and more informed have become the watchwords of our society. This book is about that. It is about living your life with caution, and building trust through thoughtful insight with the skills of a trained professional by your side. This book will help you to gain those skills and use them to find the person of your dreams, safely, in spite of the fear that grows throughout our lives.

Finding the right person and living a full and more enjoyable life could be just the prescription that this country needs to help us get back on our feet. It doesn't matter whether you are in your teens looking for your prom date, a college graduate looking for Mr. or Ms. Right, in middle-age rebuilding a life after inevitable changes have caused a relationship to drift, or in your golden years looking for companionship. Wherever you are in life, dating isn't as easy (not that it ever was) as it was before September 11th. Together we can make it as painless as possible. Trust me, after decades of helping people, I believe that I can help you.

I had served on the police force for nearly three decades. During that time, I had more than my share of harrowing experiences. I can distinctly remember a recent Memorial Day that was supposed to be the usual; local parade, hot dogs and hamburgers with the family, and a general day of festivities. I received an early morning page on my beeper. Upon calling in police headquarters, I was advised that a local resident had come home for the holiday to surprise his family. In fact it was he who got the surprise. His wife had a boyfriend and the result was a homicide and an eventual hostage situation. We talked him out and concluded that this would be a Memorial Day to remember.

After the paperwork was finished and I finally got home to my family, my pager went off again. It was another hostage situation! An Asian family was having difficulties with the cultural change along with some of the other social pressures that come from relocating to a new environment. The man of the house had taken his family hostage in his frustration. Upon my arrival, we found out that he had stabbed his wife in the neck and let her and his children go. He was held up in the house alone. After a standoff that lasted several hours, with no communications, we decided to "storm the house." I was one of the first through the rear door. I knew that I had good back-ups and the team I had supporting me were all experienced and well-trained. Within seconds after entering the house we found him hanging in the basement, the knife still in hand. This Memorial Day would go down in the history of the town as a day to remember.

Hostage situations, homicides and disasters of every type imaginable were what I came to expect every day of my life. Towards the end of my career, it all took its toll. My marriage ended in a divorce.

I thought I was prepared to enter the dating world. I am not a "bar person". I was not comfortable approaching women in libraries, grocery stores or in museums (like all the dating books advise). So, to me the Internet seemed like the best alternative. I soon found out what was happening in my newly discovered world of dating. I was a novice! There was a whole assortment of different "levels" that had to be considered.

- The first was the contemporary dating scene in general. Not having had to "date" for better than twenty years—that was enough of a culture shock.
- The second level I soon discovered as a middle-aged baby boomer, brought with it it's own unique set of experiences. The other boomers I was dating were all in the same boat. We all questioned many different aspects of our lives: our values, our situations, and where we were heading in the second half of our lives. Let's face it; we weren't in high school anymore!
- The last piece to this puzzle, or level, was the newly evolving experience of "meeting" someone on the Internet.

I had come to find that nothing in my police experience could have prepared me for what awaited out there in cyberspace—It was, in fact, a *whole New World*.

I've been, I guess you'd say, a computer and gadget kind of guy since the very beginning. Playing around with all kinds of electronics, computers were like toys to me growing up. Once I got on the police force, it was quite natural for me to become interested in all the electronic crime stopping gadgetry that was available, especially computers.

In the late 1970's, computers were showing up more and more in movies and in television, but people didn't generally understand much about them, let alone own them.

I was invited to attend a seminar on outlaw motorcycle gangs and organized crime. The information that I got there was a real eye-opener for me. The seminar leader, of course, went through all the traditional stuff; gun-running, drug dealing and other crime, but what I found most interesting was in the lecture on *organization*. It was then, about twenty-five years ago, that we were told that these crime groups were recruiting computer literate people to help them organize their criminal inventories. In a raid of a motorcycle group headquarters they didn't find guns or drugs; they found Tandy computers that were being used to keep track of which members had which talents, and where they could be reached. They were particularly interested in members who had come back from Vietnam with experience in explosives and weapons. They actively recruited anyone who could help them in their drug labs with experience working in drug companies, biology labs or chemical plants.

I knew that I had to keep up with this technology. If the bad guys had it, we needed it too!

Back in the old days, we used to communicate with the few thousand people that were out there in cyberspace through e-mail and through these things called "bulletin boards." They were like a public square where people read messages and added on their own comments; we called the add-ons *threads.* It was interesting, we all got to know each other, and sometimes-differing opinions became pretty heated threads. It all went back and forth, but no one became upset enough to do anything crazy. Basically, we were all fairly well-educated and you had to have some money and brains to play on the Internet. It was nowhere near as open and public as it is now. As life imitates art, it was a safer world, in cyberspace, and the physical world itself was much safer too. Things have changed dramatically since then, and since 9-11 in particular.

This is my story about Internet dating. It is mostly based on personal experience with additional parts based on interviews, relationships, and people, many of them friends, sharing with me some of the most intimate details of their lives. Having been a cop for nearly thirty years and having been on the "Internet" for the past twenty, I can say without reservation, "been there, done that!" There is very little that I haven't heard.

I'm sitting here in front of this computer as I've done so many times before. This time, however, I am not just writing this for myself, I am writing it with the purpose that I will be giving something to someone else. To see the words appear across the screen and see your thoughts materialize is almost a kind of magic. You show diverse parts of your heart and soul up there, and once it's typed the entire world can see it. That part of this isn't new to me. Like I said before, "been there, done that."

Your exploitations can have the whole flavor of enchantment, excitement or adventure. You can become whomever you want and your pen pal at the other end of a long; a very long, electronic path can be anyone from your high school dream date, to your prince or princess charming.

Things are different for me now, and yet, they are very similar. Since leaving behind my police career I have become a high school teacher at a vocational-technical school. I work with disadvantaged youth. I have multiple roles now, just like when I was on the police force—sometimes teacher, sometimes counselor, sometimes father figure. I always thought that I heard just about every story, but when you think that way, you are always in for a surprise. My father had an old saying that rings true more and more every day. "*If you live long enough, you will see everything,*" he always used to say. The more I listen to my students, the more I know that dad was right.

I went to Broadway recently and saw my favorite play again: *Beauty and the Beast*. It's an old story. Besides the fact that it is written in a way that causes your mind to wander off into medieval France, the reality is that the story has actually been around forever. The main character "Belle" frequents the local bookshop and borrows books, her main purpose to "visit" far off places. She longs for romance, adventure, drama and laughter, and in the end, finding her Prince Charming. Nothing has changed since the story was first written.

That entire story can be told about the literally millions of people who are now online seeking those same things on the Internet. The hopes, fears, experiences, stories, the danger, yes the danger, is all there. The excitement of first contact, the dangers of the unknown, and of course, the heartbreak all come into play.

I ended my career in law enforcement by retiring as Chief of Police. Everything you will read here is true. Of course, I have to say, "The names have been changed to protect the innocent." Actually some of the names have been changed to prevent lawsuits! Such is the nature of going public. But the stories will be real. They will, for the most part, be my stories, my adventures, my loves and my heartbreaks.

Hopefully after reading this if you learn *anything* at all, you will not make the same mistakes that I have. In that case, I guess I will have taken my career in protecting the public to the next level—a noble cause for a lifelong public servant. I'd also like to think that somewhere after investing the few dollars for the price of the book and the investment of time, I will have amused you, entertained you in some small ways, protected a part of you, by educating you, and in the end perhaps prevented a few of you from getting your heart broken and your dreams shattered.

I'll be going back and forth between the benefits and pitfalls of Internet dating. Once again, like a cop, I can hear the little voice in my head shouting, "Listen up people." Like so many drill sergeants that I have known in both police work and the military, that phrase in particular is one to be noticed. So please take no offense to my brass, attention-getting nature throughout this book—as there are just certain things that I feel are particularly important to your safety, and I need you to remember them.

The next time you see this material it might be written in your own world of experience, but instead of using ink, it might just be written in your tears.

I don't want to be a dealer in fear, but the world is no longer as safe as it used to be. The world situation has created an environment where suspicion looms in all aspects of life. It can be disconcerting that someone who seems like a very nice person on the outside may have a hidden fear within them that keeps them from trusting and growing in a relationship. But I will caution you that you have to be more careful. It is just good sense to trust your instincts and don't think that the world is kind and gentle. I want you to be safe, through careful observation.

Let's try and think like a cop from time to time, as it makes it easier for you to relate to me. I'm going to introduce you to a world where things are not always as they seem—a world where romance, power, mystery, lies and deceit may be at every turn. This is a world where your heart is the prize to be stolen, and the list of suspects can be as large or as small as the imagination will allow. Together we will explore some of the minds and motivations of the con artists, gypsies and thieves, who will, through the use of this electronic gateway, find *their* way into *your* heart. But even as you will find, in matters of the heart I've let my own guard down often enough to have fallen prey to the same Thief of Hearts.

I had interviewed, dated or otherwise met over three hundred women and several dozen men who were willing to share their stories with me. It got pretty scary at times. Between my own hapless dates and some of the stories that were told to me by those that I had dated and others, it seemed like I was venturing into some uncharted waters. I was open and honest and I wasn't used to the games that were all a part of the dating ritual. Sometimes I thought to myself that I was speaking a whole different language from the people who had been out there dating for a while. I knew one thing, though—I'd better learn the language fast!

I was used to being caught off guard, and making up plans along the way—this is the nature of police work! You had to be adaptable. It was necessary to be innovative and to adjust to the situation. This dating thing, however, pushed the envelope.

There are thousands upon thousands of people entering the gates of cyber city each and every day, a good portion of them looking for romance. This book is about those people from my perspective. It is viewing the cyber-world through the eyes of an experienced police professional in the hopes that it can be a safer place. It is hoped, that through my eyes, you will see your Internet dating experience as an adventure and take the necessary precautions that I took to make it safe and enjoyable.

Caution

From time to time, my writing might seem a little harsh, a little tough and I may come across as a sarcastic SOB. After being a cop out on the street in a pretty tough neighborhood, you can imagine that I have had to do some tough talking on a regular basis. The funny thing is that people who know me the best know that I am as nice as the Pillsbury dough-boy! However, as the crooks and abusers go, well...let's just say, I can be an SOB when I have to be. I apologize in advance if I offend anyone with my hard-line style, but I'd rather hurt your feelings than have you get hurt by someone who is a lot less concerned for you than I am.

Online Dating

There just aren't enough hours in the day. As time goes by and as we get older and older, time itself seems to slip away, through our hands and through our lives, faster and faster. Is it any wonder that we keep trying to do more and more with less and less? We are finding ourselves shopping for groceries "online", picking out new cars "online", purchasing theater tickets "online" and ordering the latest DVD's, CD's and books, all "online." Is it any wonder that we are now even finding our own true love…"online"?

In the post millennium world, you cannot be single and have a discussion without talking about the Internet and Internet romance. More and more people have "stories" that revolve around the whole concept. It seems like people who were technophobes would even break through that phobia to reach the online partner of their dreams. Just several years back, it seemed "odd" to "meet" someone on the computer. Through the miracle of television and the movies, it now seems to me like *everyone is doing it!*

As I began research for this book I was coming out of my own marriage, through a midlife crisis and moving full steam ahead into the world of cyber dating. I thought I was pretty unique. As a matter of fact it was kind of taboo at that time to tell people that you "met" online! I remember one date telling me to "Tell people we met at a business meeting." Things are changing, however, more and more people are moving to their computers to "meet", and the results are that millions of people are "hooking up" through their own windows to the world. Just as many people who are finding true love and romance online are also finding that many otherwise successful and happy relationships are being trashed because of the Internet as well.

For every story that is told to me about people who have found happiness through their home or office computers, I have heard just as many stories about people who have had their hearts broken, their husbands and wives stolen right out from under them, and their relationships ruined. I have heard of people traveling across the country looking for their one true love. I have spoken to more than one unhappy camper who picked up roots and left "everything" behind. Inevitably, they found themselves in some strange city or suburb. A place where they never would have been, if it had not been for that one "true love" they met "online."

Women are leaving their husbands, homes and children. Men are leaving their careers, businesses and lives behind—all to find the happiness that they thought they could not find by staying in the situation they were in, the place they were in, the lives they were in.

Does ANY of this make sense?

Some people feel *stuck!* The Internet is a way out for them. More and more people are going on the Internet every day. The possibilities have become endless. The danger more real!

But then again, there are countless stories of real happiness. People who were handicapped and could not get out are finding one another. Senior Citizens are finding that they have opened up, for themselves, a whole new "lease on life"—mainly because they found the partner of their dreams or at least a much-needed companion. People are going online in record numbers. Young and old people alike are finding that by investing some time and giving up small pieces of themselves, they have "connected" with another soul somewhere across time and space, to touch another's life and become more than they are, more than they otherwise could be.

So this whole business of dating, which is complicated enough, has taken a new turn into the new millennium. For some, it has become a Godsend. It has given to them hope where there was none before. To those people, the computer and the network it has been coupled with has opened doors for them to meet new people, share their lives and connect at some level with another person—in some cases to begin a life anew. To others it seems like they have been caught up in uncharted waters, the only thing that they can recognize is the signpost up ahead that reads, "CAUTION, you have entered The Twilight Zone."

It is impossible to guess how fast this phenomenon is growing and where it is growing to. Having been online at just about every hour of the day, I can't think of anytime when someone isn't sending me e-mail or instant messaging me. Having listed a personal ad myself, I was surprised one day when someone contacted me about four in the morning. It wasn't until I realized from her Time Zone that there was such a time difference. She was online in England and thought my ad sounded interesting. I would think it would be safe to say that at absolutely every minute of every day someone is out there trying to find his or her perfect match. Just knowing that, it makes sense to direct our discussions around that aspect of meeting and matching. Online dating seems to not only be what is presently the craze, but it also seems to be the future as well.

There are dangers involved, and just the other day while watching a program with my two daughters, ages thirteen and ten; I was relieved to hear that on Nickelodeon they were warning teenagers not to date anyone they met on the Internet. They also gave at least a cursory lesson on the fact that just about anyone can disguise himself or herself to be someone else online. I think it was very prudent and very good advice for everyone, especially teenagers and pre-teens. In the video store, I saw a movie advertised called "*Strangeland*" in which the premise was that there was a serial killer lurking about, who had met his targets through Internet chat rooms. Being in law enforcement, many times when reading the newspapers, my attention is brought to articles involving crime and criminal activity. With increasing notice, I see more and more "stings" involving police posing as teenagers, arresting child predators who are always luring their victims through Internet communication. The problem is, as we are all aware of in law enforcement, is that for every one that we do arrest, there are dozens more out there that we simply do not know about, let alone have the ability to snare in our traps.

We all need to be made aware of these circumstances. But we do not need to become paranoid. We read in the papers about people dying from choking on food—that doesn't mean we stop eating. People die each year from drowning in backyard swimming pools, they are not banned by people as a "danger"—and rightfully they should not be. Power tools alone each year account for countless deaths, dismemberment's, and other debilitating accidents—we all use them just the same. Every blow dryer and other such piece of household equipment carries on it big bright red warning tags "Do not use near water". I'm sure somewhere out there someone will be electrocuted for not heeding that warning, perhaps before you finish reading this very paragraph.

The home computer has become a home study necessity for teenagers, college students and adults alike. They no longer spend countless hours of travel time to and from the library. Piles upon piles of study materials such as periodicals, magazines, newspapers and encyclopedias are no longer needed. At the touch of a button the information that you need can be accessed in mere seconds. Previously, this would have taken days, if not weeks.

Overall, as a society we prosper because this information exchange has the ability to improve the quality of our lives. Not to mention that we gain time to do other things; like dating for example. Every technology has the blessings and the curse of a double-edged sword. It cuts both ways through the reward and the risk. Knowing how to use that information makes all the difference in the world. Hopefully by reading this, you will gain even more information, additional insight and even some prudent lessons that will help you. I can say from experience, "It's a jungle out there."

Police Notes—Chapter One, Internet Dating:

1. *Observation—online dating can be expedient. The array of possible partners is almost endless. Consequently, the opportunity to become a victim increases proportionately.*

2. *It seems that in and of itself "Internet dating" is a phenomena. It is now rapidly becoming "the craze", which means more and more people will find themselves jumping in, just to be part of the scene.*

3. *The observations that I made are valid because they came from my first hand experience. These are not stories. These are true life events.*

4. *For just as many people that are using the Internet to find happiness, it is also becoming an increasing source of unhappiness as it creates opportunities for unfaithfulness that did not exist just a few years ago.*

5. *It is, in spite of its dangers and ability to deceive, still a viable way to meet new people. It creates the ability to bridge distances and cultures unlike any other medium in the history of interpersonal relationships.*

6. *Anyone who ventures into the world of "cyber-dating" must be fully aware of the dangers that are out there. Although I'd rather not emphasize it, I must stress that participants approach this idea with a victim's mentality. Think that you can become a victim before you do anything that might compromise you.*

7. *In spite of these warnings, paranoia does not lend itself to successfully meeting new people.*

8. *By being careful, Internet dating, matchmaking and romance can be a very rewarding and enjoyable experience.*

Expectation

When you write a book like this you never know who is going to be reading it. Whether you are a man or a woman, a teenager or senior, this book is for you. In my case, I am a middle-aged guy, somewhere in the middle of a mid-life crisis, coming from a middle class career in a middle class town. I drive a mid-sized car and live in a mid-sized house. I was married with two kids. How *average* is that? Are you getting the picture? I'm an average guy, like just about everyone else out there, maybe just like you?

I'm writing to anyone and everyone who will listen, anyone who wants to get on the Internet and find the guy or girl of their dreams—their own prince and princess charming. Meeting people is meeting people. The focus is on the relationships, the courting rituals and the techniques used to capture the unsuspecting and sometimes even willing victims of the Thief of Hearts. Just know that whether you are straight, gay, married, divorced, separated, single, looking, not looking, male, female, young or old as far as I'm concerned (and here is the cop coming out) you are a candidate to be a victim.

I was Joe average every guy and I was a victim, not once, but a few times. Luckily for me it only cost a few bucks and a few nights out. As we get into this, though, you will see that looking for love on the Internet can have some disastrous endings. The costs can run much higher. But this is not only doom and gloom. I've made some great friendships on the Internet too. I had some great fun, great romance and really great times too. If Internet dating is done safely, it can be an adventure. I think a good metaphor would be that it's like riding an amusement park roller coaster. You know it's safe, but it still scares the hell out of you.

Life is about balance—there is pleasure and there is pain. Hopefully with the stories I'm about to tell, you will get some sense of how to navigate through this web of electronic camouflage and mitigate some of the heart wrenching mine fields that exist out there waiting to blow your hearts to bits. You have to be able to put your ego on hold. You have to be able to ask yourself some pretty tough questions. Most of all, I want to tell you all about the incredible psychology that takes place in the theater of the mind, where expectation is the chorus that rings through the performance being played before you.

This is one of many true stories.

I had a preference that developed over the years. Don't ask me about the psychological reasons for this Inner Child yearning thing. I have no clue. Was it based on a first time sexual imprint cast in my subconscious? Well *THAT* sounds really intelligent, but the truth is that I have no idea. The story is that I have a preference. In my case, my preference was for dark hair and dark eyes. My idea of the perfect woman also had really full lips, a cuteness about her, a playfulness. She could be a lady and a vamp. She was intelligent, and yet in some ways incredibly naive. She was young enough to be molded in a way that would make her *PERFECT* (I love that word) for me—and yet she was old enough to be experienced and maybe even teach me a thing or two.

I met her on the Internet and we exchanged e-mails a few dozen times. It usually starts out as a few quick *contact* connections. Something clever, like a comedian who is the best at one-liners. When you become as interested as I was in her, you try to send her something everyday. That contact becomes like a *fix* (a police drug term) after awhile. She comes back with something clever too, sometimes just showing a small part of herself—sometimes it's a little sincere. She is clever and sensitive.

Can you see this mental and emotional trap being set? E-mail is just like sending letters, except faster and with no postage. In fact, there are enough online services that are actually totally free. But what has evolved through the use of software and faster, better computers, is the whole concept of *instant messaging*—that's your real chance to *dress to impress*. If you are even remotely clever, you can really show your stuff. The problem is that when you *think* you are typing to that one dream date, the love of your life, the mother of your next ten kids, in reality you might just be pouring out your heart and soul to the entire fraternity house of Lambda, Lambda Phi.

You would not be the first or last person to bare the brunt of jokes when they find out you are this lovesick cop, attorney, nurse, rabbi, or whatever— and you just gave some of your most private experiences and personal emotions to an uncaring person who will simply cut and paste them all over the Internet. Remember this people: "*Privacy is NOT guaranteed on the Internet.*" YOUR PRIVACY!

Getting back to my raven-haired beauty…

…so it comes down to the *personal* exchange part here. Now it starts to *approach* reality. Please people, pay attention—you got her stats from e-mail and instant message chat, she is the perfect height; she is the perfect weight. You can see those dark pools of passion staring back at you from across the candlelit dinner that you have been rehearsing in your mind for what seems like a lifetime. She is perfection and her name is Sandra. Oh God, Sandra Bullock comes to mind. All that drama, action, adventure, romance. You set an expectation that she could never fulfill in her wildest dreams. But hey, this was *your* fantasy girl. This was *your* fairy tale. This was *your* dream come true.

You personalize all your e-mails now and she is no longer "FunGirl007" the screen name you knew her to be—which in itself was a fantasy enough. Think about it, FUN + GIRL + 007! She had all the right stuff. As if the mystery of Internet dating wasn't enough, you got to meet one who calls herself 007—the greatest secret agent of all time.

So, in my mind I was going to meet Sandra Bullock's sister! She *had* to be, I mean *absolutely had* to be just like Sandra Bullock in the movies (so I thought). Her name *even was* Sandra, how cool was that? I think as cool as it can get. I found myself writing her every day and the technique that I thought worked best, was to just share my daily experiences. I invited her into my life.

My job was pretty exciting—let's face it; how many people could write to this girl and say, "We had a drug raid today"? Of course I could embellish it a *little*, couldn't I? I mean I *could have been almost* shot—right? There was no need to say that the drug raid got us *only* a few bags of grass. Hey, if she wants to think it was the *"French Connection"*, I kind of like the notoriety.

In the world of Internet dating, if you exaggerate a little it's almost an accepted practice. You aren't actually lying, you see. So, each day I had in my mind this whole picture of "Honey, I'm home." I'd always ask, "How was your day?" You don't want to talk about yourself all the time, ask about her. What did *she* do? What was *her* day like? Show interest in her all the time, bringing out your own very best self for her to see. Today it could be a drug raid, tomorrow an explosion, next week a homicide. I could hold their interest all right, all with the intention of capturing their hearts.

Now listen up people; put yourself in this position. Can you imagine that million-dollar round table, real estate salesman, on the other end of *your* connection? Is he a *for real* person? How do you know? How *could* you know? How about the international diplomat who can only get online between summit conferences, and he is not *always* available (at least as long as his wife is at home). *Think about it!* Is he everything he says he is? How about the self-made millionaire, the entrepreneur, who wants to sweep you off your feet and take you away from your life of drudgery? Is this guy for real? He could be a pizza delivery man for all you know.

Listen up people; *things and people are not always what they portray themselves to be!*

So I shared parts of my day with Sandra and she shared her admiration of me—I was, after all, luring her in. Of course we both complimented each other, that's all part of the flirting ritual. If only I could get the chance to meet her and talk to her. We found out that we were "geographically convenient" a major hurdle in Internet dating. There is nothing that can cool off the jets of passion more than a transcontinental romance. Fortunately for me, my Sandra (now she was "my" Sandra) was within the 100-mile limit I set for myself. That was a good thing, a very good thing.

It was all coming together. Romance and a life of happiness were within my reach. Once I met her I was convinced I would never let go. *Even if it meant chaining her to the pipes in my basement.* YIKES! Only kidding! But please remember *that* image the next time your imagination gets the best of you! So I got up the nerve (yes, cops can be inhibited) to ask her about exchanging phone numbers. She said it was ok.

Now I have to tell you that a phone number is not all that much different than a social security number. Yes, you can change them, but they are still somewhat attached to you. If someone is clever enough, they can obtain all the information they need just by a phone number, so please be careful about that. Remember at the very least, from the *exchange* (the first three numbers), they can find out the town that you live in. Cell phones, beeper numbers and phone cards are the tools of the trade in this business, and I'll tell you all about them in later chapters. This was too important to let go right now, so I had to mention it!

So we talked on the phone. Once again, I have to insert here that I only actually knew *of* her for about a month. I didn't really know anything about her. We went through the usual e-mail exchange and instant messaging, and as we "*looked*" for each other online we felt comfortable enough with each other to exchange phone numbers.

Her voice sounded nice. Honestly, she could have sounded like *Lauren Bacall* (am I dating myself?) and I would have still loved her rough, tough voice. She actually sounded…sweet. A little tough with that North Jersey/New York accent. She was from Long Island and Jewish. I'm thinking Hmmm, Fran Drescher maybe; she's cute too. But she *sounded* like Fran and *looked* like Sandra. Wow, *my* Sandra was becoming more and more the fantasy. My imagination had now kicked into OVERDRIVE! My expectation had run off the charts!

I've been up late at night on the Internet e-mailing and chatting. I was doing Internet research on dating, going through countless personal ads, reading a ton of them. The concept was a little introspective, "what attracted me" was a question that I posed, and I was curious about what other people were attracted to. I sent for just about every book on romance and dating that

"Amazon Books" had to offer. My credit card was screaming. I thought that if I was going to write a book I should know what's out there.

So, besides the reading and writing, I was watching. I taped almost every episode of Love Connection, Shipmates, and a show I really was getting addicted to—Change of Heart. I studied these shows and watched the little nuances that tipped you off right at the start, as to whether there would be a *connection* or if this would be another *Love Connection Loser*. I made a tape of the loser's shows; some of the dates were out and out cruel. Change of Heart was the same thing. Some of those couples were vicious, and yet there was no change of heart. I learned something about co-dependency.

I'm not tooting my own horn, but it is fascinating what dynamics go into this whole dating ritual. I'll share that with you in a chapter just on the "chemistry" of attraction. For now, let's get back on track with Sandra.

There was no doubt about it, I was attracted to *my* Sandra. I would go for coffee in the morning with some of the other cops and talk with them about her. We still hadn't met. The time was getting critical. After all, if too much time goes by and you still don't meet, the fantasy becomes an obsession. That is not a good thing. So the phone calls began to go back and forth and we continued with the drill of telling each other about our workdays and the people that we were in contact with.

Sandra worked for a law firm and we shared similar interests in the law. There was the usual criminal stuff, and politics both in and out of the office. There was the regional news, which we shared because she lived close by, and of course there was always the weather—*anything* for contact. Contact was important so that this other person would not drift away, like two ships passing in the night. So after the phone numbers were exchanged it only stands to reason that the main focus would become where and when to meet.

Long Island is probably about thirty miles from central New Jersey, as the crow flies. Crossing Manhattan to get there, however, can be an exercise that would have taxed Lewis and Clark, especially at rush hour. It was about a two-hour drive for me to meet her or for her to come to Jersey. We decided to meet in Manhattan. You would think that in a city the size of New York it would be an unlikely place to try and *hook up*. That's not the case. There are landmarks that you can never mistake. I've done that before! I was supposed to meet a girl at a Red Lobster Restaurant in her township. Who would have ever imagined that there was a Red Lobster at the eastern end of town *and* at the western end, about ten miles down the highway. When you get stood up, you get disappointed and then angry. She was waiting and I was waiting. The aggravation wasn't funny and it was difficult to overcome. The online *relationship* seemed to deteriorate after that.

Back to our story…in Manhattan you can pick a place like St. Patrick's Cathedral, the Empire State Building, or if you were born and raised here you could meet in some quaint little local restaurant down in the Little Italy section. So we decided to meet at one of those places and I got there early as parking is always a problem in the city. It takes about a half-hour to forty-five minutes from my house to get there and another half-hour or so to park.

Sandra Bullock was my dream. I sat there in a sea of imagination; drowning in my own expectation, and not even realizing it was happening (a dangerous thing). I was thinking about her making some kind of a grand appearance. In this case it would have simply been getting off the local bus (do you remember Sandra in the movie Speed?) Yup, all the elements of my imagination were working alright. I knew *basically* what she looked like. The main thing I was looking for was a red jacket with jeans. I saw her coming off in the distance. But something about this picture wasn't *exactly* what I had in mind. She didn't have *dark* hair; she had *dark red* hair. Ouch, at least it wasn't as red as *that lipstick*. Talk about full lips, she looked like Bozo the Clown. Dark eyes turned into bulging ebony rivets as she stared at me. Pools of passion that I imagined in candlelight turned into murky clouded waters. The Titanic came to my mind, as my ship was rapidly sinking. *My* Sandra Bullock was actually Sandra Bernhardt. I was devastated. Superficial, no I wasn't disappointed, yes I was! If I had not built up my own expectations and met her in a bar, I might have been attracted to her. She was not unattractive. But the expectations that I built up for myself set me on a pathway to disappointment. I built a mental construct for this unsuspecting woman that she could never have fulfilled. I'll explore more of this with you as we go through the book.

Listen up people, you will see this again. Our own egos, our own hopes, our own dreams, they are the things that allow us to fall prey as victims on the Internet, because we are dealing with expectations. Do you ever go into a situation with the expectation of being assaulted, hurt, deceived, or injured? I don't think you do—and I don't think you would. In my case it was disappointment. I could live with that. I'll get over it, and I did!

Some people carry the heartbreak for a long, long time. The emotional scars can be very painful. If it's the wrong person you meet and they cannot deal with the disappointment, they can become stalkers, or even worse!

Listen up people; please learn to trust that caution is the key. Don't let your emotions rule your reason. Always trust your intuition and don't let your expectations control your own logical thinking. After that date Sandra and I never spoke again.

Police Notes—Chapter Two, Expectation:

1. *Anyone and everyone is on the Internet. To think you may not be a victim because you are different in some way would be a big mistake! Do not expect that because you are unique, you cannot be a victim.*

2. *The people who become victims of all crimes are "average" people. Expect to be a victim and you stand a better chance of not becoming one.*

3. *Within your own mind dangerous expectations build with anticipation. You need to be aware that this is taking place. It will help you from becoming disappointed.*

4. *We all have our own pre-conceived notions about people, about what we expect from them, and how we expect them to act.*

5. *Expectations of privacy are a thing of the past in the cyber-world. There is no privacy.*

6. *You can easily get caught up in a fantasy world of imagination. You must always be aware that this is an ongoing process.*

7. *Phone numbers, social security numbers and anything that identifies you can also be used to locate you. Be careful about giving out personal information.*

8. *The amount of time that you spend on the Internet and the phone is directly proportionate to the amount of expectation you build.*

9. *People are the same all over the country, all over the world. Everyone has expectations based on their hopes and dreams. There is no demographic that is unique to any one location, group or culture.*

10. *Expectations can build to a dangerous peak if they are left to themselves. You must be aware that you are placing prior experiences and a history of relationships into every new encounter.*

11. *Use logic and common sense and you will more than likely not be disappointed.*

The Players

What do you want to be when you grow up? How many times do you remember hearing *that* question? The reality is that, through Internet dating, you can be almost anyone you want to be. The facades that people paint for themselves can range from slight exaggeration to boldfaced lies. Both can be disappointing. The outright lies can be a danger. I know that sounds rather strong. I want it to sound that way because once again people, listen up—how much of a lie are you willing to accept and for how long? These are two very important questions! I can really go into a long and repetitive monologue about white lies, petty lies and the difference between lies that are committed (commission) and lies that are omitted (omission). But the real situation is simple; do you want to accept lies from someone that you are supposed to be building a relationship with?

There seems to be a *general acceptance* that prevails; if someone wants to shave off a few pounds of his or her weight, or add an inch or two to their height. Perhaps they may even take off a year or two off their age, owing the explanation to *"just rounding off."* So she's not thirty-four, when you asked she just casually said "Thirty." Apparently you didn't hear on that all-important phone call to her when she actually said "Thirty*ish*"—not really her fault, you see? You should have been listening better. I know that when I'd tell people I was a Chief of Police they just flat out refused to believe me. I supposed I could have more easily convinced them that I was a journalist, scientist, lawyer or doctor. All I had to do was keep a scientific journal on my desk or even a few magazines, and with a quick quote, I could convince most people that I knew what I was talking about. Police Chief was the *easiest* to check out. All anyone had to do was call the police station and ask for the Chief. If I didn't answer, they would know that I was lying!

Internet Casanova's come in all shapes and sizes, and they all want to capture your heart through whatever attraction they can muster. It usually comes in the form of some extreme exaggeration or clever omissions of fact—like simple things such as they are married or have three kids from their first marriage, and four from their second. That little problem of being *misunderstood* by three previous employers in the last ten months is really not something that he is sure you want to be bored with.

I'm sure all relationships have their challenges. Internet dating is no different. All relationships have problems when they start out. Internet dating is the same. But in the past when you looked into a person's eyes, drove past their house or apartment or spoke with the common person that brought you two lovebirds together, there were clues. In that respect, I have to show you a few ways to become a computerized super-sleuth. I need to be able to give you some real skills to *cruise by* their chat rooms and see what they are up to. Ways to *check them out* through the member's directory or personal ads are techniques that can make the difference between romance and heartbreak.

Some of these simple things are not very difficult to do—but they are worth the time. For example, from the first time you become interested in someone online, start printing out the e-mails and hold onto the hard copy. As you get into an instant messaging frenzy with this person, before you close that chat window, print out the chat log. After about a week or two, go back to that piece of paper and maybe ask the same question again, worded a little differently. Comparing the answers is one of the simplest and easiest ways to catch a person in a lie. Telling the truth is always easy. You remember the truth. Telling lies, on the other hand, requires real effort. You have to keep remembering which lie you told to whom.

In the case of a real player, he or she may have a few people they are working with and a few different stories, one for each. Unless they are really, really good (players), and unless they too are keeping extreme notes, then you will catch them before you can get hurt. For the mere cost of a few dozen sheets of paper and a printer cartridge, you can really save yourself some grief; at minimum save the chats and e-mails on your hard drive. That practically costs nothing, and you can use it over and over again if you decide to dump the loser.

As a word of extreme caution, some states have laws against electronic stalking. In the event that this person becomes dangerous in some way, it is very useful to have evidence. Also one last thing, if a dangerous situation should occur, early on while chatting and e-mailing, some suspects of this type will give much more of themselves in the beginning. They tend to be a little more open at first, seemingly friendly, to bait you. They are far less cautious in the beginning. You may lose evidence that you wish you saved later on; important pieces of information about themselves, their jobs or their location. It is always prudent to save, save, save.

So the question I started out with begs to be answered. "What do you want to be when you grow up"—truthful I hope. If you are serious about finding love online it can be a very happy, fun and rewarding experience—as in any new venture you must use caution. Exercise full responsibility and of course read whatever you can and talk with people who are already doing it. Hopefully you will finish my book and take the advice that I have to offer.

I didn't start this Internet dating *book* as a training program. This book was originally designed to be a combination Internet dating guide and some safety tips combined with humor and a little drama. I actually had the grand idea of writing a full novel, creating characters and developing plot lines. It turned out (and I should have known this) that once again, as I found myself drawing from my own personal experiences, the experiences of others, and a few select news items—that truth is always stranger, better and much more interesting than fiction, any day of the week. So that's why this book developed the way it did.

As I'm writing to you, I can say that this has been a real labor of love. I'd been writing on and off for over two years, dating all along the way and when not dating, at least interviewing all kinds of men and women about their experiences. Some of the characters in this book that are written as me, or are supposed to be me, are actually composites of me and others that I have known. It developed that there were some categories of shared experiences that we all had in common.

Some that come immediately to mind were the Dates from Hell and the "Falling off" stories. Dates from hell, well…they were just that. The Internet dating translation of that popular phrase is *No Picture—No Date!* A hard and fast rule that the sooner you adopt, the happier you will be, and the less time you will waste.

The falling off stories are the real heartbreakers. They are stories that started off so casually, never even hinting at a relationship, that eventually through the process of Internet dating take on a life of their own. I can distinctly remember one girl that I had chatted with and eventually caught up with in Instant Message. One night, chatting online with her until 2:00 A.M., we were talking about some *spiritual* experiences that we shared. Some involving a real personal side to our beliefs and how casually her boyfriend had been taking her in that area, he was not interested at all. She wanted so badly to just receive an affirmation that what she was feeling inside was valid. Her boyfriend just wanted to watch sports.

Well, on that particular night she instant messaged me about a dream and we went back and forth, and she was asking me for answers. We chatted and typed back and forth on and on until I realized that for about fifteen minutes, I was typing but she wasn't really answering. I paused and typed to her "Is everything alright?" She typed back, "I never felt like this before with anyone, Dennis I'm crying." It was right then and there, that reality smacked me in the face. My words made her cry. Simply the placing of my hands on these electronic pressure points that we call keypads caused her to bring so much emotion to the surface.

This was powerful stuff! No pictures, no sound, no bells and whistles, just words crawling across the screen. I knew that words were powerful. My entire career was dedicated to the power of the pen; the force of law, these were all words. But this was happening in real time. There was no legislature involved; the governor didn't have to sign anything, no debate. There were no emotionally charged hearings, no transcripts or evidence. This was simply a thought and a few keystrokes followed by another and then another and then another. And she cried and cried and cried. She wasn't saddened by what we were saying, she was happy to have the release and, more importantly, know that another human being was interested enough to stay awake until two o'clock in the morning and listen.

This Internet stuff can be very powerful. It can also be very addicting. So we became close, at least I thought so. And like so many other Internet stories regarding this whole *falling off* theme, we were supposed to meet and supposed to meet and supposed to meet. We e-mailed, chatted and even talked on the telephone. Naturally, you would think that contact had been made. Until you actually get that face to face, it's just not all that real.

Listen up people—don't lose your heart to an electronic lover, a computerized paramour, and an Internet interloper. You will get hurt, you will feel pain, you will cry. Her computer name was something " Cutesy." She was Portuguese and from a neighboring town. Once again, geographically convenient and she had that European charm. Falling in love was not all that difficult. She fit the right chemistry requirements as far as looks, age and body type went. It was all there. She even had a boyfriend that seemed to be so wrong for her.

It was worth my time and effort to pursue this microchip maven. She had an unusual name; it was like Maribella, so she could never find anything like the little license plates that you get as a key chain that would say " Maribella". I went out of my way to have a few things custom made for her. I had the little key chain engraved with "Maribella" on it and on the other side was the Portuguese flag. She was a schoolteacher and I had a few things I picked up with that theme in mind also. It wasn't expensive, just an investment in time and thought. She seemed worth it; we were so tuned in to each other. I looked forward to the nightly exchanges. It seemed she would log on the second the door was closing and her boyfriend had left. She couldn't wait to unload her day and start to *feel* herself coming out. We shared much, she laughed at a lot of what I brought to her, and there were times again when she cried. God, how I can remember her crying. After a while, we eventually exchanged numbers and began calling each other, and she opened up even more. I felt so needed.

Being a full time cop and a man who just wanted to find the *right one,* I thought I had it all together. I was a good listening ear and she seemed appreciative. We both filled each other's needs. It seemed like a good thing. As I look back through my own notes I'd say our entire "relationship" lasted about three or four months. I can now view this in retrospect as being far too long of an investment of emotions, time, psychic energy, personal resources (those trinkets) and just plain simple effort.

Don't ever get caught up into a situation like that. It's like digging a ditch deeper and deeper. Of course, all the while I was thinking I'd meet her and life would be, once again, *happily ever after.* The lesson of course is in that overwhelming *expectation.* I looked forward to her chat and e-mail each night but then she didn't write for about a week, and there were no instant messages. I thought I'd missed her saying something about going on vacation. I didn't know. I phoned and there was no answer. I continued to e-mail my days events, as if she were getting them and not having time to reply. Or, in the event she was away—when she returned she would just catch up.

Two weeks went by, and eventually three. I stopped e-mailing her. I phoned a few more times. After about a month her phone was disconnected. She never contacted me again. Falling off, the term we use in Internet dating means that she just "fell off the face of the earth." As I write this I can still feel the sting of wonderment. Of course, you always wonder if it was something you might have said or done.

You never know when they fall off. You of course eventually rationalize; she took off with her boyfriend and found love with him—or maybe she was having the same online romance with someone else and that developed faster and better. You just never know. About a year later I was near the small foreign language school she taught at and decided I'd drop by and see her. The school had closed down and I have no idea where she lives. I'll never see or hear from her again. I still have the key chain. Falling off is not a fun thing.

So that tells you about some of my own and some other types of experiences that seem to be unique to this whole Internet dating scene. I have dated in the *real world* and had continued to date both through the Internet and through personal acquaintances. I try as I talk with you in this book to reconcile the two, bringing up the pros and cons of each. Remember earlier on when I talked about the *Dates from Hell?* Well, in those cases if you can ever imagine going on a date from hell, or if you've ever just been on a blind date that turned into the most depressing and self-deprecating experience of your life, you can relate to this.

At least on the Internet you can easily ditch that experience and that person with a few short keystrokes added to your privacy options and a change in your screen name. In that case, you would want to fall off. Actually, after a really bad date, you would hope that you could push them off the face of the earth, especially if they lied. I once dated a person…well, let me start this way…

It all comes down to the chemistry thing, which I promise to talk about in great length in it's own chapter. For now, suffice it to say that looks are important in the sense that unless you are blind, you have your preferences, and even then you still will.

Let's just say that I am attracted to the height/weight proportionate. It's ok that I may be a little overweight, but, not being judgmental, I like my women petite to athletic. People on the Internet in their personal ads have some rather unique ways of describing themselves. Out and out fat men call themselves husky or stocky. Women prefer the very cute and absolutely magnetic way of slipping into their ads BBW, which stands for big beautiful women or using my other favorite "Rubenesque".

I put right out there in my own ads; "BBW's please do NOT apply." I am not being judgmental. I am just honest enough with myself to know that if it's not going to happen, why waste each other's time?

I've talked with women who loved full heads of hair, hairy backs, and hairy chests. Some said they would date a gorilla if they could get the necessary paperwork. Bald men need not apply. I happen to be graced with good thick hair; I am NOT follically challenged. I am also tall, six foot two inches tall. One woman who happened to be about four foot ten said she would be extremely intimidated by me. I am not intimidating, but I am imposing. I can understand that. She thought she would look silly or feel silly. Who was I to challenger her, and to what purpose? These were her feelings and she was entitled to them.

…And now, back to my story about one of my dates from hell.

I met Belinda online and she seemed like a sweetie—one hundred and thirty pounds and five feet eight inches tall. She had light brown to blonde hair; green eyes, and seemed to have it all together. Her hair was short and curly. I prefer long and straight. Oh well, it can grow and I can adjust. The basic body was there and things seemed to be moving along nicely. I hope that you are getting all of this because I am not only relating to you about the dates from hell concept, I am back on the letting your imagination run wild theme too.

Please people, I may be a little overbearing on this lesson, but expectations on the Internet are the worst! Anticipation coupled with expectation are deadly, deadly errors. You would have thought that my police academy training would have better prepared me for this. In matters of the heart we are all novices, and as a public servant I like to think the best of people. After dealing with crooks, thugs and banditos of all shapes and sizes, as well as gypsies, for-tune tellers, con artists and outright liars, you would think that I'd be a little jaded and somewhat prepared. NOPE, I was totally blindsided.

Belinda was not all I thought she would be, which I could accept. What really annoyed me about the lie was simply the fact that she was not at all what *she said she would be.* That's where the disappointment turned to anger. Disappointment I could shake off and move on. The deceit was alarming and just plain dishonest. For starters, her hair was not short, but rather non-exis-tent. I told her at least a few times, that I preferred long straight hair. As if that wasn't enough, do you recall my rant about the BBW's and how they are not in my "be on the lookout" list of women that I was attracted to? Well, I know that you are saying "God, Dennis, are you that superficial? How much off could her weight have been?" Let's just say that I can make some adjustments. Let's say, give or take ten percent. If she was supposed to be one hundred and thirty—thirteen pounds in either direction could be acceptable. Who weighs them-selves every day, anyhow? Well, Belinda did not weigh in at ten percent plus or minus. She did not weigh in at FIFTY percent plus or minus. In fact, she was ONE HUNDRED pounds overweight. I naturally have to mention the ridicu-lously loose fitting clothes that she blatantly attempted to disguise herself with. Even under those yards and yards fabric where it was virtually impossible to tell where the rolls of fabric began and the rolls of Belinda ended. Even under those circumstances, I had to say I noticed that she was a *"little heavier than her profile."* I still remained a gentleman. Her very innocent comment was quite simply *"I was meaning to fix that typo."* Belinda was NOT one hundred and thirty pounds, she was TWO hundred and thirty pounds; NOT five foot eight but about five foot five.

I was in shock. Truth is always stranger than fiction, and there were no places in my imagination where I could have pulled up this story that seemed like a reject from the X-Files or a Stephen King novel. We had a drink and sur-prisingly my beeper went off. "Oh well, duty calls", and I was out the door. It was one of the few times in my life when I wished I was at least capable of drowning my sorrow in liquor. I really envied the intoxicated at that moment. I immediately went to a Barnes and Noble and purchased about a hundred dollars worth of books on dating. You know those *"Dummies"* books. Boy did I feel like a dummy. You'll hear this again and again until you get it right peo-ple: NO PICTURE—NO DATE!

Needless to say, Belinda and I never spoke again either!

Police Notes—Chapter Three, The Players:

1. *It seems to be generally accepted that people lie on the Internet.*
2. *It is especially true if people are "talking" about themselves. They seem to think it's OK to lie, because they are presenting themselves in a more positive way.*
3. *Sometimes people lie by leaving out important details. Not telling the truth does not only mean saying something that is inaccurate; it can also mean not telling the whole story.*
4. *It is always best to check details and ask the right questions. Knowing how and what to ask beforehand prevents a lot of misunderstanding.*
5. *Print out everything! It is an invaluable resource later if you have any question at all if the person is telling the truth.*
6. *Compare notes. Take some chat logs (printed) from weeks before, ask the same questions, and compare answers.*
7. *You have to know yourself and what you want before you go on a quest for a mate.*
8. *The people you meet online are REAL people. They can become very special to you, or very dangerous. Don't think because you have not met them, that they are merely computer-generated personalities. They are real and have feelings.*
9. *What you do, say, type, print or communicate to your online buddies can affect them positively or negatively. The computer can be a powerful means of communication that can change lives. You become part of that process when you go online.*
10. *Sometimes people just "fall off." As in real life, you can have your emotions twisted by players on the Internet.*
11. *Players on the Internet come in all shapes and sizes. The amount of happiness you get and give can be directly proportional to the amount of honesty you share with another possible mate.*
12. *No Picture, No Date.*

Relationships

There is something to be said about relationships. After listening to more than 500 books on tape and reading countless books in print, I can honestly say that I thought I had a handle on them, *thought* being the operative word.

When you spend nearly three decades of your life as a public servant, you encounter all types of people in all types of situations, many of them high stress. I've had the occasion to see people at their best…and their worst. Nothing that I encountered in police work however, can compare to some of the experiences that I had *on the dating scene*. The relationships stories that I heard or experienced were a world *all of their own*.

I posted personal ads on several dozen boards across the United States, looking for anything unique to the east coast, or any other part of the country for that matter. People are the same all over, especially when we are talking about them looking for a real relationship or even true love. I ran a few "test ads." Some portrayed me as a knight in shining armor, you know, the type of man who would just come along and sweep you off your feet. The women who read them probably imagined that I would appear on their doorstep and take them away from all the problems of their world. I had to reach way back into my past and pull up a bunch of key words in order to compose these ads, simply because they weren't me as I am today. It wasn't all that difficult because I remembered from my Boy Scout Oath that we had promised to be trustworthy, loyal, helpful, friendly, courteous, kind, obedient, cheerful, thrifty, brave, clean and reverent.

I actually used those words to "bait" the ad and see what kind of response I received. Basically I got a lot of women who wanted someone who, in their mind, was a "pushover". Upon getting their number and speaking with them on the phone, I had to be honest with myself and say, "Dennis, this would NEVER work." I mean, it *was* me in the sense that I was a "nice guy", but, it wasn't me in that I certainly wasn't a doormat either. Women who are attracted to the mamby pamby types want a man who will be nothing more than a trained dog on a leash. There is something unnatural about being "too nice" in dating. I know from eavesdropping on the women's audiotape books and from reading

"Cosmo" and the other women's magazines that it is all talk when it comes to nice guys. In fact, when dating, nice guys *always* seem to finish dead last.

I am the stereotypical nice guy. My mother and I had a good relationship; I was the "baby" of six kids, so she and I bonded very well. In addition, I had three older sisters, and a lot of aunts on both sides of my family tree that treated me well growing up. My issues with older women were virtually non-existent when I started dating.

All through my teen years, I can distinctly remember nothing but being in normal or functional relationships. I had my ups and downs. There were girls I liked that didn't like me, and there were girls that liked me, that I didn't like. I remember that in the seventh grade two "girlfriends" of mine, Linda and Eileen, were both at my house. Now admittedly, they were higher up on the maturity ladder than me. It was obvious that they both had a serious puppy love crisis going on for me, and all along I thought it was pretty funny. One Saturday it came to a head when they got into a physical fight over me and Linda took the chewing gum out of her mouth and put it into Eileen's hair. It was hilarious to me but not to them. Eileen had to cut chunks of her hair out to get the gum out. I never dated either of them, one of my life-long regrets, as they were both so cute—and I just wasn't getting it.

As I got older, I was pretty fortunate to never hook up with anyone who really used or exploited me. For the most part, I was always generous as I came from a big family. It seemed like the right thing to do, to share my time, my attention and whatever I had with my girlfriends and guy friends.

I came from a distinctly blue-collar middle class family and was always encouraged by my mother and father to treat people with respect and to give what you had when you could. Being generous was natural for me, and it really helped me out when I got older. Little things like a pack of gum or a simple gesture like picking a flower from the neighbor's garden and giving it to a girl, went a long way. I never had anything that I can remember that would put me into the category of an abusive man or a user. That's why this whole dating scene thirty years later and the concept of being a player is absolutely fascinating to me.

I also have to say that in some of my ads I got a chance to play the part of the *bad boy*—wow did THAT open the floodgates. I could never have imagined that so many women would be attracted to a man who seemed, and I must say this, borderline abusive in their own solicitation ad—and here is the real kicker. The younger girls in their twenties seem to be the ones who objected most to my sarcastic ads. The older the women were that were responding, the more they were "in love" with this bad boy. You would think that after years of dating and countless failed marriages they would want the kinder and gentler sort of character. Put a personal ad out there that says words like "confident," "no BS," "take charge", "personally in control", and the ever popular "high self esteem", and they come flocking around you like bees to honey.

I put out an arrogant and nearly abusive (in my opinion) ad all across the country—on at least a dozen different personal sites. It was pretty nasty; it was about being "all that" and more. The ad spoke of being an accomplished man who's no BS style has brought him to the top. Let's get to the point here, I cut the sincere and sensitive stuff and found out what women really want. They wanted tough, strong, and lots of attitude.

My God, they came running. I couldn't keep up with the e-mail. I even ran a bunch of ads without a picture. It didn't even matter how I looked. I had one woman from Texas who wanted to fly to New Jersey sight unseen and take me with her on vacation—they love the bad boys.

As I began to analyze it, there is a two-fold attraction to the *bad boy* type. The first is always the passion. There is no way that the nice little boy next door type with the neatly trimmed hair and the horn-rimmed glasses is going to sweep you off your feet on the dance floor, at the family re-union, or in the bedroom. It's just not the image these women share. The second, and it's right up there in priority, is that many women have been beaten, scared and abused by their former husbands and lovers. I hate to have to say this but…they want a strong man to protect them.

Of course there is always a certain portion that equates love with violence, but I'm not talking about the dysfunctional here. I am talking about the average everyday woman, whether she is single and working, student or mother, she wants that man who can pick her up and literally carry her away. Again, it rings of the man taking her away from her troubles.

I know that there will be throngs of independent women out there who will probably be screaming when they hear this. And believe me, I feel bad that I have to say it, but they are the women who after decades of NOW, women's rights, and the whole women's liberation movement, are in the distinct minority. Actually, they wind up being the women who cry the most.

Almost every man that I talked with during my interviews didn't want anything to do with "that type." The men wanted to be protectors, and at the most, they would accept a woman as equal. No man that I ever interviewed said he would be comfortable with a woman who he thought was "superior" to him. Yes, the concept is there, and they would probably say that they think strong women are admirable. But in reality, none of them would want to be married to one, and their answers to the contrary would only be because it was the politically correct thing to say. How sad in this post millennium world, and after almost a century of women's progress, the glass ceiling of relationships is more intact than ever.

I am pondering a thought that the only woman most of us men wanted to be strong was Mom. Now let that thought run through your mind. She was the only woman we ever wanted that could fix anything, make it better, keep the bullies away and bring our weary heads to her tender bosom for comfort. Do we subconsciously want anyone else to take her place? I don't think so. Exactly what are we thinking about when we think of a strong woman? What image comes to your mind? It has to go back to those pre-teen days when mom was our one and only. I can't see myself getting all too excited thinking that woman is every bit as strong as my mom. And WOW, do I want to date mom? These are two incompatible thoughts and feelings.

On the other hand, there is the conflict going on where every little girl's hero is her Dad. Who could be stronger, who could be more handsome and who meted out the family discipline? When the woman that you just met sees your STRONG side, what comforting thoughts come rushing up from her inner child? I am playing psychologist here, but I'm also telling you a lot based on my observations. I've worked with family crisis for more than twenty-five years. I've read hundreds of books, and I have studied this stuff. In my present role as a high school teacher and resident role model for many young women, I feel I am more qualified than ever to say these things. It's not anything that can be stated as unequivocally correct in any situation. But I can say this; statistically the women I've met overwhelmingly want a strong man. However that message is conveyed, either physically or verbally, it sells itself every time.

To all my women readers, you have to read between the lines here, too. Every man is not going to write like a poet or have the writing skills to convey that his thoughts are pure, his intentions are noble, and his heart is in the right place. This whole Internet dating thing has brought about a revolution in writing skills and thrills. In other words, the level of gamesmanship has moved from what was the typical classroom note passed among adolescent schoolmates, to inter-office e-mail. The difference being that in the past you could simply look across the classroom and see who was sending the note and pretty much get a "read" on whether it was worth your time and effort. Now your computer paramour may be halfway across the continent. What you read is not necessarily what you get.

So my responses to these ads kept coming in every day. I can begin to distil the ads into an actual magnet for what I am looking for. It's a great process because as you begin to play with the words you can target your ad in much the same way that advertisers set up market test groups for their products. There is no end to the new players in the game coming on board every day. It's not like the online women have a club where you are going to be found out. That's just not going to happen. In the United States, every single day, thousands of people are buying computers, thousands more are just beginning online services, and of those thousands, countless more are finding their way into Internet dating relationships.

I'm sure I am not the only man to figure out this stuff or the first person ever to "fabricate" an online personality to suit the situation. It all goes to the honesty and integrity of the individuals in the game. I ran an ad in which I was "brutally honest". It was totally me! It said I was an author, that I was writing a book about Internet relationships and that I had been an accomplished man with worthy goals and high ideals. I was there for the taking, so c'mon ladies, get in line for this once in a lifetime opportunity. Of course I am being both succinct and somewhat entertaining here for your benefit, but basically that was how it read. Of course I got back my usual responses from all the women that wanted a successful man, but there were a few who thought I was so "terrible". I was called a "braggart" and "of myself." That wasn't the case, I was just…well…being me. However lacking in eloquence I may have been in my ad, I can truthfully say that I didn't have on my humble face the day I typed it. One twenty-nine-year-old from Philadelphia, a pre-med student said it "made her ill". I wrote back, "it's a good thing then that you are in pre-med." She didn't reply.

I've had so many phone conversations as a result of my efforts to bring about this book. So many women, so little time. Chemistry always comes into the mix. Most women start with some trepidation because I am a stranger. It's always a little bit awkward in the beginning, but second to exhibiting strength is the "humor factor". By and large the single best icebreaker, scene-stealer, get your foot in the door taker is the ability to get them to laugh. By putting a smile on their face and a warm glow of comfort in their heart you get to take home the prize ninety nine times out of one hundred. Looks are important, but they run a distant third to strength and humor.

Police Notes—Chapter Four, Relationships:

1. *Just when you think you have relationships figured out, you can count on getting surprised.*

2. *From my own experience, people are looking for more out of relationships than just a comfort zone. It helps to be daring on the Internet. There is too much mediocrity and you have to stand out from the crowd somehow.*

3. *On the Internet it's possible to create fantasy relationships. The problem comes about when you have to fulfill that fantasy.*

4. *Some people, believe it or not, will travel just about any distance for love. This has become increasingly more evident on the Internet.*

5. *Every person is not a literary scholar. You shouldn't judge entirely on written ability or content. That is all only a part of their online skills, not their personality.*

6. *Sometimes the more gregarious and flamboyant you appear in your Internet personality, the larger than life you seem to be. This is one of the elements of establishing Internet relationships, at the start.*

The Personal Ad

If you are at all serious about dating, you must consider the personal ad. Whether it is through the Internet or not, this is probably the best way to, well…advertise. There probably are as many types of formats to consider as there are places to advertise. Examples include your local newspaper, and then you might upgrade the circulation base by taking out a regional ad in a local or national magazine. Of course, the type of magazine would indicate somewhat the type of person you are. It would be ridiculous to take out a personal ad in say, *Field and Stream*, if you absolutely hated the outdoors. I guess some of this is pretty obvious.

Another type of personal ad might be the type that you place in local college newspapers or in selected periodicals. Trade type journals would include the arts, legal or medical profession or even club magazines. As I said previously, the possibilities are endless. In some publications, there are pages upon pages of personal ads…of course, some places don't even have them. Nothing says that you can't be the first. I don't know if Field and Stream takes personal ads. I'll say this; if you wanted that big, burly lumberjack type man beating a way to your door, or more likely chopping a path through to your heart with his chainsaw brute strength, you could be the first to place that ad. There is nothing like holding a monopoly in a pool of candidates. Although you might be the first, I'm sure shortly thereafter you would no longer be the one and only. Good news travels fast!

On the Internet all you have to do is run a search of *"personals + free"* and the floodgates will open. There are many free "trial" services as well as just plain free services. The difference being that the totally free services want you at their site, because of the advertising that they sell. On the other hand, the pay services are a little bit (not much) more professionally run and the candidate pool might be slightly (also not much more) upscale. Some of the Internet dating services that I have encountered offer free postings for females, but for whatever reason, men must have a credit card.

There are a number of highly expensive and selective personal dating recruiting firms popping up. I would add that for every one of them starting up, there are just as many going out of business.

In case you were curious, the fees for these services start at around one thousand dollars and go up exponentially from there. I must say that one thousand is NOT typical. It is the very lowest end of the spectrum. In fact, typically these services cost several thousands of dollars. The better of them actually do a background check, along with a personality profile and guarantee some kind of result in some form. This might include numbers of dates or a time window with so many "connections" provided.

There are many services that start out well, but due to either insufficient advertising or unrealistic expansion plans, the cash flow dries up and then, of course, it becomes a problem keeping offices open, and before you know it the system collapses. What that may mean to you is that the three or four thousand dollars you invested looking for your *someone* special becomes money lost. The whole "matchmaking" business works as only a combination of a numbers game—and a shell game.

You absolutely (this variable cannot change) must have a continuous supply of "fresh meat" coming through the system. As long as that happens, there is cash flow and there is at least a *potential* (key word) for matchmaking to take place. The candidates (natives) begin to get a little restless when they plop down several thousands of dollars, hoping to at least purchase a chance to meet the person of their dreams—and after months and months of no contact, frustration begins to settle in. Some of the candidates who were frustrated in the beginning are now absolutely devastated. It would be an understatement to say that their own self worth becomes mired down in rejection. There is nothing more deflating than not even being able to pay someone to "check you out".

There is no doubt that the pay as you go services have definite advantages. Probably the best feature in the service is that most of the people in the system at least had the ability to muster up the several thousand dollars required to get into the service. Quite honestly, people who pay that kind of money are *generally* not in it for the play. For the most part, they are more serious about finding a relationship and not just a series of dates. That's probably the biggest plus about the system. One suspicion that I had about these high priced services that I couldn't prove, but seemed quite possible, was that the operators of these services had *purchased pictures of models* to use as bait. I noticed that when asking these services for samples of people who had subscribed they had dozens of beautiful (model looking) professional women seeking men *just like me!*

What a surprise when I asked a few of my female friends to make the same inquiries, they were shown countless pictures of *model looking men*. From talking to several men and women who were disappointed with the service, they all said that when they attempted to contact the *prospective mates* that they saw at the service, *none* of them were available. In fact, the only people that replied to them, or contacted them, were just everyday people much like themselves. That is not a bad thing! But let the buyer beware. If you are shown dozens and dozens of great looking people by the sales representative for the service, ask yourself this, what's wrong with this picture? They may quite simply be rented faces to lure your money—into their pocket.

For the more average and cost conscious person, the Internet offers proba-bly the best coverage for the best price; in short, the most bang for the buck. The caveat is however, that although you get the most exposure, you also have the least control. Personal ads have been known to take on whole new identi-ties whenever some mischievous prankster gets his hand on your bio and your photo. It's a risk. It's not a big risk and ad sabotage is not prevalent, just some-thing that I wanted to make you aware of.

Online personal ads take on all shapes and sizes. They started out in the olden days as singles bulletin boards. These were merely listings with interest-ing titles followed by descriptions of the eligible bachelors and bachelorettes. In time, as new graphics packages became available, photos were associated with the descriptions, and online personals became more and more popular. You must be ever more careful of identity theft, though. Putting out too much information can be dangerous. You walk a very fine line between telling about yourself, and exposing yourself. Be prudent about how much information you give to people. Even supposedly "reputable" services have the ability to sell this information.

As I began to frame out the outline for this book, I was in the middle of my research and was constantly "tweaking" my online personal ad. Summer was officially coming to a close and with my "new and improved" ad I could see that it was now time to let the games begin. Summer vacations were over and everyone was returning in droves from the lakes, shores, and mountains across this vast country. It would now be even easier to find that certain perfect some-one right here in my very own Pentium Paradise. There is invariably more to choose from as summer sun makes way for autumns, cooler and colder weather, rain and eventually snow. The tendency to find your recreation on your home computer is obvious as the shore booths and mountain lodges close up for the season.

The situation with some of the girls I met during the summer gracefully passed on into the short-lived history of computer romance. There seems to be a definite correlation between the increasing speed of computers and the ever-shortened length of online computer relationships. Everything keeps moving faster and faster and faster! As speed increases and the need for multi-tasking and efficient use of time increases, the players who make a habit of "meeting" online have learned quite efficiently to streamline that part of their lives as well.

In talking with women during the summer, it became clear to me that a pattern was emerging that enlightened me to their "grazing process". Actually, some referred to it as their "shopping" process or even "window shopping." Some called it browsing while others just simply stated that it was "cruisin the personals." It was something that I could certainly relate to and wasn't unique to the opposite sex.

Sitting comfortably on my bedroom chair complete with pillow, soft drink off to the side, scented candles burning and portable stereo cranking, I prepared myself to compose yet another personal ad. This time I was going to experiment with a rough and rugged persona. I've created an entirely new screen name, called up the web sites of a few free personal ad services and I am ready to roll. To get me into the right mood I dig up a Country CD and now I am poised and ready to show my best face to all the women out there hungry for a "real man." My opening line was—"If it ain't country, it ain't me."

While I have one foot in the cyber-world, I need the other foot in reality to make the whole process a *real* experience. Actually, what I am meaning to say is that I need the whole process to be *believable!* I looked through about twenty or thirty personal ads from women that I printed out earlier in the evening— each and every one was an arm charm date. I needed a persona to lure them away from the countless others that were out there vying for their attention at the same time I was. I needed the edge and the country music provided me with just the right mood.

The problem is that when women are scanning the ads, you have only a few seconds to make an impact—to get them to stop, look, and listen. That's why ad construction is critical to online romance and crucial to the online player. I thought the whole country and western profile would be a good way to attract a woman who wanted a "real man".

Let's face facts, am I being too superficial and putting too much emphasis on feminine desire? Am I really far off base to say that most red-blooded American women want their own boy toys as much as the men want the arm charms? From every woman I talked to there was a resounding call for "real men" who seemed, from my conversations, to be in short supply.

I can't answer why—that seems to be all psychology—sociology stuff, I just know the stats. Overwhelmingly "real men," was a major criteria in my study!

I met a girl online when I was doing the research for this book, and we had a few dates. She was nice and all, I guess you could say she was the *date of the month*. She came into my life the same way all the others had. I either saw her personal ad posted somewhere in cyber-space or I found her in the member's directory. Then again, maybe she replied to any one of my personal ads. Whatever the case, we connected ONLINE! In any event, I sent her a note and, although this may sound impersonal—she took the bait! There was, of course, the whole courting ritual, the e-mails, the Instant Messages, the online chat, then that fateful day we exchanged phone numbers. After that, the rest was simple; we just made a real life date! Almost every girl that I had dated I'd told about this book, and that some of the things that happen with us, or that we talk about, may someday wind up here.

Every one of them wanted to feel that in some way, they are different, that all the player stuff is about everyone else except them. They are all unique in their own way. They truly are all different, yet how can I say in this rising tide of ever mounting data that they hold any place special. Players don't identify that way with their dates—and there are scores of *Internet Players* out there. In all honesty in the end, each and every one of the girls I dated on the Internet have been reduced to a series of colored folders, now filed away, and used as research for this book.

I guess if you could ever imagine looking down into a stream or a brook and seeing the schools of fish that swim past, they might appear as a wonder of nature for the moment, neither of them having any more identity or individuality than the others. They are there—just there. They swim past you doing whatever it is that schools of fish do. As you move past them, they are gone, and you move on with your life. It is really (almost sadly) such an appropriate comparison to some of the online lives I've touched throughout my research. It gets bad when you can't remember the names or even match the names with the faces. It all becomes a blur of humanity. I knew this process would have a dehumanizing aspect to it. I could never have imagined how deep it would go. I ask myself, "*names?*" I might as well have assigned numbers to these wanton women looking for their own version of Mr. Right! The imagery that I have in my mind is frightening when I think about how many times in the past that we have turned people into merely numbers. They become nameless, faceless numbers in line, waiting…waiting…and wanting. They are waiting for love and wanting a relationship. Can you imagine that? They might as well be waiting for enlightenment, salvation or to hit the Powerball lottery for that matter. The question is: can true love be found on the Internet?

Keeping in mind that over the years, insurance companies, banks, credit card companies and business in general have already reduced business at first to punched cards, and then just numbers on a computer screen. Now it was being done on a much more personal level. A very important point I'd like to make about Internet safety is that the criminal mind makes the same transformation. Criminals do not see you as a person, they see you as just another number—translated into dollars—in their pockets. Although Internet dating can be fun, connecting and personal; keep in mind that everyone doesn't see it that way.

Post 9-11 dating has taken on an additional dimension. I used to see personal ads that *proudly* boasted their national ethnicity. Foreign sounding names like Muhamed, Ishtar, Rumen and Omar have changed. The names have become so much more *vanilla* flavored. In ads that have a personal picture, the names are now simply Joseph, Bob and Dave, typically *all-American names!* All of a sudden, it's more chic to be an American, even if you're not. Names can be deceptive. Think about it.

I know that sometimes my observations may seem to have a ring of callousness. It's better that you should learn from my experience than being brought to slaughter through your own ignorance of what lurks out there. There are players out there who want to coax you, want to entice you, want to deceive you with their words. I am showing you in pure unvarnished, raw, completely honest, and open language where those words come from, and what's behind the words themselves. The thought process and emotions that come through my writing are for you to take and hold ever so close to you. Hold them close so you can understand that no matter who it is, the best and the worst of us can be hurt and can hurt others. After years and years as a street cop I can say with complete authority…"It's a jungle out there."

Police Notes—Chapter Five, The Personal Ad:

1. *Personal ads are your advertisement. You should select a place to put an ad that is consistent with the type of person you are, or the type of person you are attracted to.*
2. *There are countless free web sites to post a personal ad on the Internet. You must consider, however, that sometimes, you get what you pay for!*
3. *Just because you pay a lot of money for a dating service, doesn't mean that you are going to get satisfaction. Sometimes the more you pay, the more frustrated you can become.*
4. *If you are looking for the most exposure for free or for your money, the Internet has virtually unlimited coverage.*
5. *The variety and selection of possible mates on the Internet changes by the minute. The personal ads also change just as fast.*
6. *Not only is the ability to post an ad incredibly fast and comprehensive, the ability to scan personal ads is equally as efficient.*
7. *It is best to create a mood when composing your ad. It should reflect a particular style or personality and be consistent. The clearer the ad is, the better your response will be.*
8. *You can paint a picture with words in your ad that will, in fact, present a very realistic picture of yourself. This helps you to find the type of person who would be attracted to someone like you.*
9. *It is always good to scan other ads and see the way others have presented themselves. If you are not particularly good at writing, you can borrow some ideas that you liked in their ads.*
10. *Expect that the process can be de-humanizing. When you post a personal ad, you do become part of the herd. You need to know that being out there also opens you up to criticisms and comments about your ad.*
11. *When composing your ad, you can maximize your positives and minimize your negatives. I recommend, however, that honesty is always the best policy.*
12. *It's a jungle out there!*

Chemistry

Chemistry is an elusive concept. When you "meet" people on the Internet, as in real life dating, there is always a certain amount of chemistry that must be there.

Whether you choose to use email, instant messaging, personal ad's, telephone calls, faxes, voice mail, online photo ad's, or even video dating...no contact is the same as sitting across from the other person and just having a conversation to establish chemistry! The best measure of honesty is still looking someone right in the eye and watching what they do as you learn about them.

Usually most people will say that chemistry refers to liking a certain "type." From all my research and from my own personal experience that is generally not true. There really is no certain type of person at all. There are, however, *preferences* that we generally tend to be attracted to. If you get a chance to really get into people's heads about their preferences, you might find out the same things that I did in my research. There really aren't any preferences either, that is, when the *chemistry* is right. Most of what I've learned about the subject of chemistry has nothing at all to do with the physical attributes of a person. It has to do more with the *attraction* that one person has to another, based primarily on how the interaction between two people seemed to evolve.

Physical attraction is an important part of chemistry. It is usually one of the first criteria in establishing who matches up with whom. I can say from my own point of view that I've sat across from women that most people would consider gorgeous, however, once the conversation wasn't there, the chemistry rapidly was lost. The recent movie "Shallow Hal," is an excellent example of the superficiality of many people when first meeting. It is a good commentary on everything that matchmaking is not supposed to be when based purely on physical attraction.

I think that there are some things that seem to attract some people to each other that can't be defined. Some people will have certain gestures, little quirks in their personality, or they may do things that are just attractive to act as a magnet to most people. On the contrary, there are also some things that people may do that are somewhat repulsive and should set of alarm bells. Chemistry really is a *combination* of so many different things, that we can analyze it best by going through it step-by-step.

The first thing to do when you ask yourself, "*What am I attracted to?*" would be to ask first, "*Do I know myself?*"

As you read this, you might get an uncomfortable feeling, thinking about how you might have to self-analyze yourself with complete honesty. It isn't easy to do.

As I looked through the thousands of personal ad's in the nearly five years of research for this book, I can honestly say: I am stumped for a definition of exactly what I am attracted to.

A good, quick clue emerges as you begin looking through personal ads, and computer matchmaking services for the "profiles", of possible connections. In those profiles a new term in interpersonal matchmaking has emerged. It is taken directly from the world of computers and that term is: KEYWORDS. They quite simply and directly sum up for you in single words the characteristics of what you think you might want in a mate.

This is a good practical exercise.

The words that come to your mind first, the words that you scan for in the personal ad's, can be very telling about what is important to YOU! Whether you know it or not, the qualities that you say that you are looking for might be very telling about the type of person you are. In order to find the personal happiness that you are looking for, you must know yourself first!

- Is physical attraction the first thing that comes to mind or is it character traits such as loyalty, generosity, integrity or honesty?
- Is it more important to you that your future partner has a certain "look," or behaves in a certain "way?"
- Are you looking for tangible features first and foremost?
- Are you more interested in qualities that can only be measured by performance and the way your mate will interact with you?

Of course, every one of us wants it all. We want the total package. But no one person can be everything—to everyone. A common mistake that many people make whenever they are looking through personal ad's, or in this case, searching the Internet; is to look for someone very similar to themselves. Sometimes it is very important to realize that although someone may be quite different from you; that person may bring to the relationship what you need.

One of the best helpful hints that I can recommend works for people who have just started dating, or for people who have been dating forever, but still haven't gotten it right. It is what I call the "top-ten list."

Take some time and write down (in no particular order) the top-ten qualities that you look for in a partner. In doing this, and in the subsequent revisions, you will learn much more about the type of person that you are. By
carrying the list on a small card in my wallet, when I was dating, I would realize that what I initially wanted wasn't *really* what was important to me. After a
while you can prioritize the list in top-ten order; and then of course make dele-
tions and additions depending on what you find to be most important to you.
In the end, looking at my first list and my last, I left five behind and added five
new items that I never thought were all that important.

"One man's food is another man's poison," is a timeless expression. In dating
and meeting people, you will find these words to be extremely accurate. There is
someone out there for everyone. You might just not have found each other. It is
very true though, that what your friend thinks is the total package, would be a
nightmare relationship for you. That's why *fix-ups* don't always work.

Let me give a few short examples about setting your priorities.

If you were just coming from a relationship in which your trust was vio-
lated, you would quite naturally put loyalty at the top of your list.

If you are that type of person, for whatever your own reasons might be, you
may want to spite your former mate. In that case, you will be looking for an
arm charm to be showing off when you are with the gang. Your former partner
might be saying that they broke up with you. You, on the other hand, might
want to convince your social crowd that YOU were the one that did the breaking up; because you wanted to *trade up*!

In cases such as these, when your trust is broken and you've been hurt, it
would be understandable that you would want to have a partner who is very
loyal, and more important, very nurturing. This new partner might be very
available and nurturing to help heal your emotional wounds. But as your
wounds heal and you grow emotionally from the experience, the whole
dynamic in what is really important to you will emerge. Nurturing may not be
a long time need of yours. In the first case above, the *arm-charm* might turn
out to be quite expensive and not at all worth showing off to your friends.

In the end, what you may soon come to realize is that the nurturing quality
that you embraced has now become suffocating. What was once a nice comfort
zone of security and caring has now become overpowering. The lesson that
you learned was that there is a fine line between *Mothering* and *SMothering*!

Although I admit that I am not a psychologist, during the course of my
career I had to do more than my share of what we called *Street Psychology*.
Taking from many, many experiences where I had to intervene, offer advice, or
talk down someone from doing something self-destructive; I've learned quite a
bit about why people do some of the things that they do. Based on that experi-

ence, I've learned that in most cases *what* we do many times has to do with *where* we are in our lives.

The dating *Chemistry* that I've been talking about in this chapter has to do with our individual preferences, and it has to do with our needs. Depending upon where our lives are depends on our needs at the time.

Let's talk for a minute about the first chemistry that takes place when two people meet. Generally our preferences are what influence our first impressions. We have our likes, and dislikes, for body types, colors, features, and any other physical attributes, based on experiences in our lives that brought us to where we are right now. If we just left a job where a nasty boss was an older person, we might think that the *problem* was caused by a generation gap; that's why we quit or got fired. You probably wouldn't want to work with another older person for a while. It's the same thing in dating relationships.

People come in all shapes, sizes, colors and features. In some cases for someone looking for a relationship (I am not talking about one night stands), will be very discriminating about what they are looking for. Some people will *absolutely* not date a smoker for example, or a member of another race or religion. In other cases, you might make some compromises, trading off good points for bad points.

Here I have to offer advice on taking a few minutes to think about that top-ten list that I talked about earlier. It might be a good time to take a few minutes and get that started, or think about your first revisions.

We can begin being quite subjective. In varying degrees, we place our values on such things as hair color and length, height and weight, clothing style and manner of dress, and any one of a thousand things that can vary in degree such as contact lenses (in any color you can think of) or glasses. Whether your date smiles too much, or not at all; we begin to look into these very changing characteristics and start our judging process. Sometimes what we see is not really the person at all, but the person that we are projecting them to be. Many times the person we see is merely a mirror reflection of what we are all about at the time.

Have you ever been in a bad mood and thought, "The whole world sucks!" Well I am sure the eight billion other people all didn't suck, but from your perspective it may have seemed so. The reality, *your* reality, was based on your attitude at the time, and what you were projecting out, being reflected back. It would be really unfair for you to say that your date, a person you might not really know at all, had an *attitude problem*. Especially if during your conversation all you did was complain about was how you got screwed over in your last three relationships.

The word *chemistry* when used in this sociological context, means that there is a relationship between two people. More accurately, it means that there is an interaction between two people. These interactions can be altered by the way in which you direct the experience of meeting someone for the first time. In most cases when you meet someone new, if you smile, they will probably smile back. It seems really simplistic, but it works. During my police career, it was safe to say that in better than 90% of the time, when the police arrived at the scene, the people involved *expected* us to be nasty or to have an attitude. I have diffused thousands of irate citizens with a very disarming smile. By being polite and in some cases even humorous, I've saved thousands of people from the pain of dealing with the police in everything from a motor vehicle accident to much more serious events in their lives.

Laugh with your dates. Even if the chemistry is not there. Turn a bad date into a good date by laughing about some formerly bad experiences and open the door to a smile, even when you don't feel like smiling. You may not get more dates, but you may find a few new friends.

Internet dating runs backward. What I mean is that in *real life* dating, there is usually a physical attraction from the start, unless you are on a "blind date," arranged by some well-intentioned friend or relative. This is not the case when the only attraction that you have, at first, is a personal ad and maybe an online photo. In *real life* dating you see the person first, and get into their heads as time goes on. In Internet dating, you usually pick their brains by a series of emails, instant messages or eventually phone calls, before you actually get to see them.

As we discussed earlier in the chapter on expectation, this can become dangerous to you and it is well worth repeating. If you took that lesson seriously, however, you already know not to let your emotions rule over your reason. At the risk of repeating myself, I want to stress that the wrong thing to do would be to let a whole set of expectations work on you and create the opportunity for disappointment, all of which is never a good thing.

Chemistry in personal ads

Over the years I've become a matchmaker for quite a few of my friends. This has resulted in me also becoming the reigning "guru" for helping some of them write personal ads. I hate to admit it, but I've also coached them with their emails and even chat sessions. If you are reading this for yourself, or for a friend, sometimes that is what needs to be done to help get them (or you) started.

I can think of an example that comes immediately to mind. A close friend of mine, Bill, was going to be venturing out into the world of Internet dating. He was asking me a lot of questions and I could tell that he didn't have much success in getting the chemistry going on his own. He seemed to know what he was looking for, but what was going wrong for him was the way he was describing himself. He was getting more and more frustrated, and I knew that he really needed my help. We started by listing all of his good qualities and we came up with a really terrific ad. It was all truthful, it was just that I described him differently than the way he would have described himself. This, in turn, put him out there more accurately, and he had better online chemistry.

Another example is a friend JoAnne, who had me give her ad a *look-over*. One thing immediately struck me in the ad, something that she and I discussed at some length was when she described herself as an *earthy individual*. I queried her as to her choice of words. And I talked to her about the immediate chemistry that took place when I imagined adding that type of person to my life. Of course I knew JoAnne, and she wasn't earthy at all in *my sense of the word*. You see, JoAnne was an outdoors type person, hiking, fishing, boating and anything that had to do with wildlife (important note here: wildlife differs *greatly* from wild—life.) My interpretation of the earthy reference evoked a no makeup, no bra, untamed hair, sandals and gauze skirt kind of sixties look.

You have to choose your words carefully, and you have to put together a friend or two to help you make the ad as realistic as you are. In taking the time to do that, you will be better assured that the chemistry the ad evokes is much more what you are looking for. It's always good to have a second or third opinion, just to be sure that the message that you are sending is the same one that others are receiving.

So here is the precautionary part of this message. Be truthful, be clear, but don't be too complete. Keep your guard up. Know that the person reading the ad that you've placed now knows what you like and what you are all about. It would be great if everyone was honest and forthcoming, but that isn't always the case! The whole purpose of me writing and you reading this book is for safety. You need to know that there are some unscrupulous people out there who will read your ad and try to get into your head. In my business, I call this a *baited response*. In other words, knowing what is important to you and just what you like—someone can try to gain your approval *and your confidence* by coming across as being *just like you*! It is then much easier for them to gain your trust, mainly because you are honest; and since they are so much like you, they must be honest too.

This is all part of Internet dating chemistry. How people portray themselves, how you interpret their words, how you interact with each other electronically rather than physically—can really impact your life—both positively and negatively. It really depends on some amount of luck, in connecting with the right person, and—a high degree of skill—such as mastering some of these techniques; to filter out the wrong person.

I'm quite sure that in the future we'll see some college course on the emerging dynamic of electronic psychology. I know for a fact that every day there are scores of law enforcement officers working in this very area trying to pose as young boys and girls to bait child predators on the Internet. My purpose in writing this book is to give you the same tools that they use—the mindset of a cyber-cop.

Some of the best friends that I've made on the Internet turned out to be people that I had some *bad dating chemistry* with in the beginning. What I mean by that is that there was no *romantic* chemistry. When we eventually met there might have been something about the *look* that we didn't like, or perhaps the whole romance component was off. Because we had been honest with each other from the start, and we genuinely had very similar interests, it was easy to become…and remain friends,

Since our first contact, and in the weeks that followed until we finally met each other, we didn't waste all of that chemistry that we had developed. In several of my interviews with people, a strange chemistry developed that I think is worth sharing.

Of course before I wrote this book, some people were getting it *right* on their own. That's how this book came about; finding out what works and what doesn't. Some of the people told me stories of people they met on the Internet using the whole honest and forthright approach. They then developed some strong ties and some solid chemistry with the people they met. However, when they finally got around to seeing each other, *in person*, the magic wasn't there. Here's the strange part—because they had formed friendships, they introduced their Internet friend to another of their single friends, who then wound up dating. So you see, the different types of chemistry that can occur is really a matter of your approach to Internet dating and your skill level. That's why I think the police notes part of this book is vital to anyone who is meeting people on the Internet.

It's good to be cautious, but you have to meet people and connect somehow, and the Internet is certainly one of the best ways if it's done right.

Recently divorced, widowed or just out of a relationship?

I can offer some tremendous advice that was given to me after years of being married and eventually divorced. Date, date, date—short people and tall, big people and small—date them all. Get out there and start connecting with people—find out what you want in a relationship. For recently divorced or widowed people, I can tell you it's not the same dating world out there that it was ten or twenty years ago.

Reading some of the personal ads, going into a chat room, corresponding with other people and eventually meeting in person can be a real experience. But you need to get out of the house and meet people. You need to have the ability to connect with people at all levels, friendship, confidant and romance. I wouldn't want to compare dating to being on a *job*, but if you haven't done it in awhile, you need to get experience. For some, it may seem too easy. I know from interviewing dozens of people who were in long-term relationships that started dating again; a large majority of them had been rebounding. They clung to the first or second person that they met—looking for the same comfort zone they had in their previous long-term relationship or marriage. After a few months go by, however, they changed, and they became intolerant of some things that they overlooked in the beginning. The chemistry or the dynamic of that relationship changed. Unfortunately, most of those situations wind up being very disappointing to the people involved. It's better when you can think about it before you get caught up in it. Chemistry is a very important part of dating, you must know how it affects you and the people you connect with.

One last anecdote about chemistry—

I once went to a career counselor who had me do a homework assignment. He had me go home and write in one, two or three pages what would be the perfect job for me. Not the job I was currently doing, and not what I thought I'd like to do. He knew that if I could design my own job and could be really satisfied at it, his client would be happy and I would succeed. It was a simple enough conclusion drawn from a simple enough process. I recommend the very same for you. Take a few moments and do that before you begin to try and date on the Internet or anywhere else for that matter. Take some time to write one, two or three pages of what you want in a partner; or make a top ten list like I use.

With that description in hand, write your personal ad, and when receiving responses ask THOSE questions, and have enough self-confidence and self-esteem to bend a little here and there and really stay solid where it counts. I can guarantee that you will find yourself having more and more dates where the chemistry brings it all together for you, and for your date.

As I said before, I could someday write a whole book on Chemistry. The psychological stuff, all the physical attraction stuff, all the romance stuff. It's really simple in the end. It all comes down to:

• How much self esteem you have
• How well you know yourself
• Where you are in your life
• What you want and need in a mate.

Defining those questions early on can make all the difference in the world.

Police Notes—Chapter Seven, Chemistry:

1. There are no types, there are preferences. You have to know what you want first before you start your online search.
2. Physical attraction plays a major role in chemistry.
3. Being honest with yourself first, and deciding what type of person you are, makes it easier for you when you want to attract someone who will like you for the person that you are.
4. Keywords or buzzwords in online personals are some of the first things you will look for when trying to see if there will be eventual real life chemistry between you and your mate.
5. Everyone is an individual and what someone else may find attractive—you may very well find revolting.
6. A lot of what you "need" in a mate can be traced back to what you needed as a child. That is where many of your comfort zones are established.
7. It is important to know if superficial qualities or internal characteristics are what you are most attracted to.
8. You can easily be intellectually attracted to someone on the Internet only to have the chemistry disappear when you meet. That runs contrary to real life relationships where you may be initially attracted based on physical appearance only to find out you have nothing in common.
9. Keep away from all types of Chemical enhancers such as drugs or alcohol. These things become motivators on the Internet as well as in real life dating.
10. Just because you may have some initial chemistry based on a personal ad, it is no guarantee that will continue, personal ads can be very misleading if not downright dishonest.
11. Just because there isn't romantic chemistry doesn't mean you can't establish an online friendship.
12. Bad chemistry can result in an explosive situation. If for some reason things don't seem right, you are far better off passing up this relationship. Wait for the right one.

Addicted to the Internet, into the mind of an Internet Addict

It's 3:00 a.m., God, am I tired. I'm really dragging, just plain dog-tired. I think I'll just get a quick shower and then right off to bed. I know that I have to be up at 7:00 a.m. I'm thinking, "Four hours sleep, that should be enough." I like taking a hot shower before settling in, it relaxes me. Coming home these late hours I can't afford to toss and turn. I'm just getting in from Linda's house. She is really nice, twenty-eight years old, five feet ten inches tall and a svelte 130 pounds. She has raven black hair and a complexion that would make a china-doll green with envy. I can't stop comparing her to Jaclyn Smith. She's my Charlie's Angel all right. The water in the shower is really hot, especially hot tonight—probably because it's been so sweltering outside. The heat wave we have been having across the whole country has literally been a killer. The late night news is talking about nearly one hundred people dead in Texas alone because of the heat. It's been hot here too—very hot. I mean from the heat cooking off my computer screen. Linda and I met a little more than a month ago. She was pretty wonderful, I mean nice and well—wonderful. I can't help but notice the hesitation in my voice, and in my thoughts. I think it's because I'd like to say, "She's perfect." But in reality I know she's not, maybe close, but certainly not perfect! Perfect, as a matter of fact, may just happen to be right there, just a few short steps away from me—waiting for me.

I really hate this, you know? It feels like I'm addicted to this whole damn computer gamesmanship, the whole art of *the play*. "Damn" I say, "I'm jumping right into the shower and then off to bed, no computers, and no getting online tonight." As I walk towards the shower I think, "I'll check my e-mail in the morning."

The shower cascades down my back. It is so refreshing, a combination of relaxing and being restored. I use this herbal bath wash to really rejuvenate me. I am feeling better now; the problem is that I know what's coming next. I'm doomed, absolutely doomed—to getting out of the shower and hitting that damned keyboard. My emotions really get jumbled about now, between the late hour, and the time I have before going to sleep, I'll take a chance to see what I might find in the online personals.

All my hopes, dreams and aspirations begin to tempt me closer and closer to turning on my computer and just getting into the game for a little while. I ask myself, "Who knows?"

I know that in turning on this thing I might just find someone new who might be all the more perfect for me. Things were going well with Linda, and this was just one more complication in my life that I really didn't need now. "Why was I actually doing this anyway?" I asked myself over and over. I always arrive at the same answer—perfection. Finding the perfect person, my soul mate and my true life's partner. I rationalize by saying, "Who could pass up a chance at perfection?" After all, I should only be online for a couple of minutes.

The biggest fear of all computer players is that for whatever reason, they suffer that God-awful fate of digital disappointment. What that means, quite simply, is that when you turn on your computer there is NO e-mail, that is to say ZERO e-mail, none, nada! This is the true wrath of cyber-space! Once having turned on the computer and having no e-mail you immediately have that sinking feeling of being unwanted. It's bad enough that to many of us cyber-space has become a real place. At least a real place in our minds. The worst possible fate one can imagine is to have no place in a place where there, well…let's face facts…where there really is no place to begin with. I know I'm sounding redundant! I know I'm really, really tired. This whole introspection thing is killing me. I have way too many questions concerning what is going on in my life right now, and most of it seems to center around this computer! I'm getting the feeling that the best thing to do—for me right now—would be to simply dry off, turn this damn thing on, check e-mail and go off to bed. I mean, thinking about it, how long can that possibly take? I'm guessing a few minutes at the most. Right?

As I dry off from an especially refreshing shower, I power up my little Vaio laptop. It whirs on with it's usual routine of clicks and beeps. Off to the side the printer path clears itself and out pops one single sheet of paper. The Windows screen comes on in my very familiar "desert" color scheme and wallpaper. As I am drying off and throwing on a loose fitting pair of sweats I patiently wait for that all too familiar hourglass to stop spinning. It finally stops—I sit there for a moment—staring at that blue-green America Online icon. Of course I don't waste one moment of time as I click on it to begin my ritual. In the short time it takes to connect, I busy myself so it doesn't seem like I'm actually waiting. I do some quick chores around the desk straightening things like piles of paper and a few other desk items. While I'm doing, that I keep one eye on the screen.

I see my computer connecting, interacting with the service. Now it's checking my password, the final step. The first thing you hear is a booming "welcome," which is meaningless, that's NOT what I logged on for. I'm anxious for the next three magic words, which I hear within the next few seconds "YOU'VE GOT MAIL!" "YES," I exclaim, as I get the feeling that I am reborn once again. At least my citizenship in the world of cyber-space has once again been validated.

I'm in cyber heaven as I scroll down through my e-mail. Ten, twelve, wow, it just keeps on going. I have about twenty pieces of e-mail. A quick glance however reveals that most of it is Spam mail, the Internet version of junk mail. I whiz through them being very careful that I might accidentally delete something that is actually personal mail. As it turns out it's all a bunch of the usual junk solicitations. Porno, Porno, College Co-ed Porno, Make a Million on the Internet selling NOTHING, (God how I HATE this stuff), more porno, even more porno. So my e-mail finishes off as usual, about fifty to sixty percent solicitation for porno sites (the Internet version of 900 numbers) and about another thirty percent of some type of pyramid, multi-level marketing, or other type of get rich quick scheme. Of course friends (and I use that word dubiously) send a regular supply of stupid chain letters and jokes. I can go through a ream of paper a week on stupid online jokes.

So now the fun part, Babe Watch Millennium Style. I have had a few personal ads running here on the Internet across the cyber community. I'd like to tell you at least a little bit about them in case you might be interested. One ad ran in an astrology matching area: "Find your soulmate through the stars." It seemed to be a bargain at a mere $8.95 a month. That was of course if you paid one year in advance, otherwise it was $12.95 per month. I had a PHOTO-AD running with a service called "Match-Something.Com. That service proclaimed to be the Internet's largest database of eligible bachelors and bachelorettes. The price for Match-Something.Com was a mere $11.95 a month, not too expensive a price to pay for a chance at perfection. Of course since I already subscribed to the "largest" database with Match-Something.Com, I also had to subscribe to the Internet's "fastest growing" database at LoveCity.Com. As it turns out for about thirty or forty dollars a month, not counting the $19.95 that I was paying for America-Online, I managed to get a pretty steady supply of female candidates for myself. I find a little irony on the wording of all that too, after all they really are Candid-dates. Here in the dark corners of the cyber-world, nothing is what it appears to be.

So as I looked through my real e-mail; all the non-junk mail, there was some of the usual stuff. Of course, by the time I got home from Linda's there was a nice "Thank you" from her. There was an online "kiss" (an electronic type of greeting card) from Michele in Queens; I can always count on that, my long distance love Carmela from Texas sent me some really nice e-mail. Then of course there were all the damn jokes, jokes, jokes.... I must be on a dozen of my friend's joke lists. I just delete them; as I said before, you can go through reams of paper printing them out. Really, most of them repeat themselves anyhow; they seem to keep making the rounds. Then there was—Hmmmm, a new one! It was from LUVLYLADY. Let me click on this and see what it has to say? I'm curious, at least a little. She put nothing at all in the subject line, however the e-mail reads:

Dennis, I saw your personal and it sounded like me...) I'll copy my personal here...and attach a different photo than what is in my ad (I'm on the left, last Halloween)...If you're interested, please e-mail me!

Isabella

Her personal ad was pretty much what I'd been looking for. It was interesting at this point, age: 33, Location: Upper Hudson Valley, NY. I thought quickly for a moment, about three hours away. That was geographically convenient. Sexual preference: straight, which was good, no hint of anything crazy. And then she went into her narrative, half oriental and half Spanish. "OOH-LAH-LAH, what a combo," I thought! She is five feet, five inches tall and she weighed in at a nice 125 lbs. A great combo, a perfect size, and she seemed to love all the same things that I did. No wonder she said my ad sounded so much like her. She liked Sinatra, Jazz and Blues, Old Movies, Hmmmm; she was sounding better and better all the time. She also attached a photo to the text file: GENIE.JPG. I thought for a brief moment, "Where the heck does the Genie come from?" Then I looked up again, "Oh yeah, Halloween pic." So I clicked on the download photo icon and waited. I really wanted to see this one! As it downloads I look to the corner of the computer screen on my desk and see that The digits are inching closer and closer to three–thirty AM. "Arghhh," I groaned as I thought "a half-hour online already." I figured I'm still within my limits, right after I see this photo I can still manage to get three and a half hours sleep. I figured that sounded like a plan. The picture is downloading, 15%, 25%, 35% I can see the top of her head, then her eyes, she looks OK so far. She had really dark, really nice eyes, scratch that, she had drop dead gorgeous eyes. Her hair looked really dark, almost black but definitely dark brown. The picture continued to scroll down the screen. It was now at 45% and I was looking for that smile. I love a great smile. At 55% I saw a GREAT smile, a super smile, world class, big and bright, great teeth, it seemed like this had all the possibilities of a good thing. The last half of the picture though was the real test. As we began the second half of the download at 55% I was now anxious to see her body. I had seen one hundred and twenty five pounds turn rapidly into two hundred and twenty five pounds in these pictures. I am not into larger women. As the picture continued to slowly pace itself vertically down the screen after 65% and then 75% it was obvious she was everything she said she was. In a word she was ALL THAT! Now realizing of course that it is now past 3:30 a.m., I felt I'd make the time investment and write back. At least I thought about writing back. It was really late. Then I thought again, "Damn I can't let this fish get off the hook." I thought as long as I am asleep by 4:00 AM, that would work for me. I thought I might as well make this one work, she seemed like she would be worth the effort. I also thought that it is apparently flattering when a woman wakes up early in the morning and checks her e-mail and she sees that you took the time to write back.

Writing back is usually pretty simple, if it's not someone that you really want to make an impression on. But this one—"LuvlyLady" was a woman that I didn't want to make any mistakes with. So as I thought about it I knew I had to write something INTELLIGENT. I thought, "Women love that." Then I thought I should put in something complimentary. Not too obvious though, that can seem like a player just looking to make points. Flattering yet subtle is the way to go. I had to put it all together without sounding like I was desperate or like I was a dork; both of those, being the proverbial Kiss of Death. I thought it was best to start out with all my stats. I typed in that I was 6 ft 2 inches tall, and I added that I was a pretty tight 225 lbs. OK, OK so I am actually 235 pounds, but everyone fudges a little bit on their weight, don't they? I told her that I worked out three times a week. I was going to joke around that I only worked out one week out of the month though! Then I thought "NO," if she believed me, or it came across as stupid, I was history. I thought to myself, "Play it straight Dennis." There was something about this one that said No BS…I continued that my hair was kind of light brown in the winter but got much lighter in the summer, when I'm out in the sun. I always type that I have chestnut brown eyes, just a little extra instead of plain old brown. I looked up at the screen where her picture was still there, now downloaded at 100%. It was easy to get lost in my own imagination; those dark black pools of passion in her eyes were staring back at me, right into mine. It was hypnotizing, or I was falling asleep, one or the other. I felt that I was losing myself into the fantasy. It wouldn't be the first time I thought pools of passion, in reality I could meet her and find out she was cross-eyed. Yup, it would not be the first time that my expectations exceeded reality. I thought about this one though, this one seemed to be different. Of course you always want that one to be different, to be perfect; that is after all, what the goal is here. I knew perfection could be within my reach. In this case, Isabella had something about her that spoke to me. I said to myself, "Take it slow Dennis." Investing time and some sense of intelligence here, things could just work out.

MY INSTANT MESSAGE WINDOW POPS INTO MY E-MAIL...

PinkLady: Hi

DenisJrsey: Hey!

PinkLady: Busy?

DenisJrsey: Never too busy for you. (*Which was really not true at all, because right now I was focused on Isabella. I didn't need the interruption, but I thought that I owed it to her. After all, I did just spend the last weekend at her place*).

PinkLady: I had such a great time with you last weekend, can we do it again?

DenisJrsey: I'd love that idea, I was hoping we could do it again, and again and again. (*I joked, but actually I was hoping that she would get offline already. My attention was drawn not to her, but about a hundred miles north up the Hudson valley*).

PinkLady: You were so nice, I think this could really work.

DenisJrsey: It can if you want it to (*the only thing I wanted was for her to leave me alone for now*).

PinkLady: I was really nervous about meeting you and all, you made me feel so comfortable.

DenisJrsey: I have that effect on women, LOL (*Yeah, laughing out loud alright, I have to get back to this e-mail or else I'll never get finished, and I didn't want Isabella thinking I blew off her e-mail to me*).

DenisJrsey: I was just checking e-mail, I am really exhausted, can we talk sometime later on this week?

PinkLady: Of course sweetie, you know I'll be looking forward to it!

DenisJrsey: Me 2, G'Nite.

PinkLady: Sweet Dreams

DenisJrsey: Nite

PinkLady: You know I'll be dreaming of YOU!

DenisJrsey: Me-2 (*Yeah, maybe, just maybe TOMORROW, because I won't be getting ANY sleep if you keep this up!!*).

PinkLady: I'll let you go.

DenisJrsey: Thanx.

PinkLady: Nitey Night Sweetie

DenisJrsey: Bye.

I was dying here. It was now past five a.m. As I looked at the window through the cracks in my room darkening shades, I could see the early morning sunlight starting to peak through. I am really hooked on this stuff; nearly daybreak and I still hadn't finished my e-mail to Isabella. I quickly clicked on my privacy preferences and blocked ALL instant messages from EVERYONE. I didn't want any more interruptions! I thought and thought I needed something that had an "edge" to it. Something that would set me apart from every other guy looking to get her attention online.

The ratio of men to women on the Internet is probably three or four to one. However, the ratio of hound dogs or scrubs to eligible women, that is to say guys who are constantly on the prowl for the very, very few women is probably one thousand to one. I am assuming of course that just about every guy is out there looking, searching, hoping, some even stalking. Guys just "trolling around" looking for what they might catch in their love nets. Of course loving women the way I do, those sainted creatures, I naturally assume are here swapping recipes for dishes like meatless corned beef hash or perhaps comparing notes on responsible subjects like the correct way to raise their children. I am taking on the assumption that a small portion of the women online actually are here looking for dates. Of course I'd also assume most quality women wouldn't want too much to do with many of the computer geeks anyhow!

How I arrived at these assumptions is quite simple. I have interviewed literally hundreds of men and women and they all seem to share pretty much the same experience in their Internet dating stories. The women upon posting an online personal almost immediately get their mailboxes completely stuffed with responses until they are actually full. This translates to the fact that most Internet service providers put a limit on how much server space you can occupy with your personal mail. My Internet service, the last time I checked, would store up to two hundred and fifty pieces of unopened mail. After that, the sender gets a message returning their e-mail, that the mailbox is full. Other service providers may be more or less liberal depending on how much they charge you for a monthly fee. The women I have interviewed have literally complained that their mailboxes were jammed to full with men begging for dates. Their main complaint being that they couldn't get their regular mail from their girlfriends, family, friends and other seriously interested parties. Some were even forced to change their screen name to stop the onslaught. It is really very easy to get lost in a crowd as a guy, unless of course you are quite clever.

Men who have ads online get an average of between two and four letters a day. That is only the case if you list among the information in your personal ad this long list of required and supplemental information:

You must send your total stats, which would include your age, preferably your date of birth (girls want to know what "sign" you are). Your height, weight, eye color, your chest, waist, and buttocks size (girls love cute butts). Also what would be helpful, now PAY ATTENTION gentlemen, if you want a response to your personal ad you should consider including the following:

Your FBI fingerprint classification codes, for background checks. Your social security number, next of kin's name, address, and telephone number and include the relationship. You might possibly include a scanned in copy of your birth certificate and the front cover of a current passport, a copy of your social security card. As a matter of fact, scanned in copies of all your credit cards. In addition, you could provide electronic filing copies of your last three federal income tax returns, complete TRW and Equifax credit report profiles, net worth and income statement updated within the last six months, recent appraisals on all real estate owned. To be completely politically correct it would also be helpful to provide notarized affidavits that:

You are not now, nor have you ever been a member of the New World Order, any subversive group advocating the violent overthrow of the United States Government, a Multi-Level Marketing genius, a salesman for Herbal health products, a representative of any company selling "magnetic" health products or any type of machinery that either juices, blends food, processes fruits, vegetables or extracts the nutrients from any plant, animal, or other product.

Once you have given all of that information to your prospective mate in your personal ad, you might, yes gentlemen; you just might get a response. I don't make these rules, I just observe them.

Now to really make your mark and get you into the driver's seat, you might want to consider an online greeting card, available from American Greeting.Com for a small monthly fee; available online, of course. Another approach that might be flattering would be to send her any number of gifts. For example: How about a nice music, video or DVD, available from CD-NOW.Com. You can order it online using your Visa card, MasterCard, American Express or Discover. CD's may be purchased starting at about $14.95. Another nice touch might be to send a romantic novel to her. Just in case you have difficulty expressing your love, you can let a professional do it. This is really simple, all you have to do is contact Amazon.Com, the world's largest online bookstore. They would be competing of course with the OTHER world's largest online bookstore. That being Barnes and Noble.Com. As a last resort there is always 1-800-FLOWERS.Com which can be sent to her. Once again, charged to your plastic cyber currency usually starting at a paltry $29.95 and up.

So the question is, how could I compete out there in the world of cyber-meet-marketing and get the attention of LUVLYLADY. Well, as a player, you have got to know the "deal". You have to know how to sweep them off their little cyber feet and get them to notice you. One foolproof method is COMMONAL-ITY. You have to speak their same language. You can forget about the Mars and Venus stuff here. In cyber-space those planets may as well be off in a different galaxy. In acting class 101, the first rule you learn is *play to your audience."*

You wouldn't go to the opera and sing Country and Western music, would you? Nor would you go to a country jamboree and start bellowing out Rap, not unless of course you wanted 200 bottles of Iron City beer thrown at you.

So to get her attention, I had to resort to time-tested tactics! The good old reliable member's directory. If I was lucky, she said some things there about herself—details that weren't in her profile. There may have been some details that she may have long since forgotten that I can pilfer to make a great impression. In the member's profile, you can really conjure up a mixed bag of tricks. I have seen some women put in the bare minimum first name, state of residence, astrology sign. Others really pour out their entire life's history; children's names, occupations, jobs held within the last ten years, exact dates of birth of every member of their families, who to notify in case of death or serious bodily harm, their most recent last will and testament, the list goes on and on. I think you have the idea. It can be anything from their favorite chili recipe to the combinations of their safe deposit boxes. These are people who sometimes have no one to share intimate parts of their life with, and they post the information in the hopes that someone, anyone, will pay attention to them.

Listen up—identity theft is the fastest growing crime in the United States. Please be aware that everything you think you are posting privately on the Internet can very easily become public knowledge.

So I checked out LUVLYLADY's member's directory profile and found:

Name: *Isabella*
Location*: Upper Hudson Valley, NY*
Date of Birth*: September, 1965*
Status: *Divorced*
Hobbies: *Chardonnay's, Rieslings, motorcycles, working out, traveling, fine dining, enjoying the finer things in life.*
Computer: *Sony laptop*
Occupation: *Paralegal*
Quote: *Obviously you have no mirrors.*

Well I thought, "Not too much to go on." I had to work with what I had…Hmmm. Let's see…She obviously likes wine, maybe I could tell her I'm a member of Alcoholics Anonymous. No, that wouldn't work, perhaps she would be wanting to belt down a few and she would be feeling guilty. Hmmm, I see she like motorcycles. She didn't say if she was into just motorcycles or HOGS. That would be Harley Davidson's, the sign of a true motorcycle enthusiast. This is substantially different than the occasional Sunday driving owner of any number of rice burning imports commonly known as crotch rockets, mostly made in Japan. I was really thinking harder and harder here how to use what little information I had.

So I darted off my first e-mail reply to Isabella AKA: LUVLYLADY.

It went something like this:

> *Intelligent professional looking for the perfect woman. Our first date would consist of riding my full dress Harley Davidson to a wine tasting festival. After that we would find a fine French restaurant where we could while away the hours talking about future vacations together to all the exotic places that we could think of. We would also run along sandy beaches and work out to a sunrise exercise class along the coastline of some of the finest resorts the world has to offer. When we were finished with our workout we could have strawberries dipped in fresh cream and take in all the museums, theatre, and all the local cultural events that our vacation wonderland has to offer. If you would be interested in helping me plan a future date and possibly work together planning a dream vacation, please write back.*
>
> *Sincerely,*
> *DenisJrsey*

So I covered all the elements: motorcycles, wine, fine dining and travel, and of course I also covered what I thought that nebulous expression to be, which she listed as the "finer things in life."

Well, my reading and playing audience, if you actually believed that I sent that e-mail and that Isabella would actually respond to such obviously deceitful tactics, well then this book is working for you. If for one moment you got caught up in all the BS of my fictitious reply, you are certainly a candidate to get taken in by an online player.

Listen up people, you have to know that people do this sort of thing. In fact, I did reply to Isabella. She e-mailed me back and after a few e-mails and chats we exchanged telephone numbers. I'd have to say that her and I talked on the phone, perhaps at least three, sometimes four or five hours in a night every other night for a couple of weeks. Our phone conversations were so much fun we were both exhausted all day long. Rapidly becoming zombies, we decided to meet. I traveled up the Hudson to meet her, and we had an absolutely amazing weekend together. The funny part was that the chemistry was just not there for romance. We became really great friends though. We now e-mail each other every so often, mostly around the holiday weeks, and we talk on the phone once in a while.

Police Notes—Chapter Eight, Addicted to the Internet

1. *It can be psychologically addicting to get on the Internet and look for online relationships. A dependency can develop in which you seek acceptance from other members of the online community.*

2. *Introspection and a strong desire to become part of chat groups and other on-line adventures (role playing and fantasy) are very real reactions to becoming involved with Internet social clubs and organizations.*

3. *There are hundreds of services available in which you can meet people, many are free, and many that cost exorbitant amounts. Use caution when contracting with any online service.*

4. *Many online services (dating, matchmaking) boost their memberships with free trial offers but do not have a large regular database in which to choose from. Make the most of the trial period to determine if you want to subscribe to the service. If you get no replies during the trial period, paying a user fee won't help much more.*

5. *Always ask for a picture before agreeing to meet. Print two copies, leave one with a trusted friend or relative. If the person who shows up doesn't look like the picture, abort the date!*

6. *Whenever you are in instant messaging, it is always possible that the person you think you are talking with is entertaining several conversations at the same time. Never assume that you are exclusive.*

7. *There are any number of services that are screaming online for your credit card information. Do not be so anxious to impress an Internet mate that you carelessly purchase items or products such as flowers and greeting cards. Be sure the company and your newfound friend are not one and the same.*

8. *Anything you put into the members directory becomes an easy gateway for a stranger to gain your interest by saying that they are interested in the same things you are. They can use your own information to exploit you.*

9. *Developing friends on the Internet is a good thing, developing co-dependencies on the other hand is not. Do not become an Internet addict!*

Tools of the Trade

The tools of an online player are the same that any real life player would use. These are the items that enhance his or her ability to keep in touch with you safely, escaping your detection.

Listen up people, there are players out there. They want to be in touch and they want to be able to get to your heart. But the ability to track them and have accountability is an ever-elusive battle between wits and technology.

I'd like to make you very aware of some of the things that you might encounter, so that you can think about just how the game is played and also so that it won't be played on you. Obviously, we are going to focus on the computer and communications. As you enter this world of cyber dating, it's pretty obvious that both of you have a computer and both of you have at least a telephone line. The problem comes in with the service. Going through a server it is nearly impossible to tell the who, what, when and where about anyone.

Back in the old days of DOS based systems, there was actually a built in safety factor. In the old days of CompuServe, whenever a new person would log into a chat room you could tell which NODE they came in on. That meant that you could actually tell at least within a few miles which service line brought them into the server. I could easily see if the person chatting with me was from New York, New Jersey or across the country for that matter. I used to log in from a Central Jersey line, and all of us from Jersey knew the other Jersey designations. Well, so much for your history lesson. That is no longer the case so it becomes almost a moot point.

As you begin to converse online with others, of course you will be asking them some personal information. You should be able to develop enough of a rapport with them to have them give you some certain pieces of information that will tell you more about them and put your mind at ease. If anyone is reluctant to tell you about himself or herself then you should approach with extreme caution. I went on a date with a girl whose screen name was Lydia12345. She answered a personal ad of mine and we started to e-mail back and forth. Of course, I naturally assumed her name was Lydia. After a few misses online, back and forth, we eventually caught each other in chat. So we chatted for only about two or three days when we decided to exchange phone numbers. She asked me to call her later at night and I figured that perhaps she had children that she wanted to put to sleep. She was only about thirty minutes away, so I knew that there were no Time Zone considerations. People don't usually think about those things, but on the Internet you can literally wind up chatting with someone around the world.

So I called Lydia, probably three or four nights in a row, when she said to me that her name was really Angela. OHHHHH-KAYYYYY I said—having felt just a little bit stupid and getting used to calling her by what was the wrong name. I had called her and she called me back a few times. I never thought to check on the caller ID to see if the number I was calling was the same number she told me to call. I should have checked the exchange too, but I didn't bother to see if it matched the town where she said she was from. Listen people, you may see this again. CHECK THOSE NUMBERS! Numbers are just like names and addresses, they can tell you a lot about a person. Once or twice I called her and got her answering machine (so I thought). It turned out to be her voice mail system. Well, whenever we talked she seemed really nice, actually extremely nice, perhaps too nice. I did break one of the main rules of Internet dating, however, and just to show you how real this all gets, even after writing nearly ten chapters of this book, I fell prey to my own carelessness. She didn't have a picture and said she was really in great shape. She said she looked athletic. She was supposed to be five feet ten inches and about one hundred and forty pounds. Ok, so that all works for me. I was going to meet Angela, who was supposed to be athletic and was supposed to be really nice.

So we met in person at a public place, it was a T.G.I. Fridays, Now I never meet for dinner, because if they turn out to be anything other than what they said, I have a drink and get out of there. Thank God for experience. So we met at the bar and she was anything but athletic. That is of course unless you consider SUMO wrestling a sport, albeit one not very popular here in the United States. She wasn't oriental, so it just didn't figure. OK, so we had the drink and we were talking. I made some small talk, but it was obvious that she had lied about her appearance. She had lied originally about her name. Now I had just found out that all along she was using a cell phone number. The reason she wanted me to call after 9:00 p.m. was because she had it set up that after that time she had free unlimited nights and weekends. Now in the conversation she is extremely nervous and trying to ease the tension somewhat by telling me a humorous story. As she is telling me this story, she is saying "My girlfriend was so funny, she said to me just the other day—she said Alex, let me tell you…" at that point I said, "What did she say?" Well now Lydia or Angela or Alexis or whatever her name was said "Well my name is Alexis Angela but my friends call me Angela." Of course I wasn't going to let that one go. I said to her, "Well then why in the story you were just telling me, your friend said Alex?" She realized she was caught. At that moment I didn't know who she was, what her phone number was, where she lived or even if she was married or not. If she was taking any type of precautions, she blew it. After that there was nothing she could have told me that I would have believed. It's OK to be careful, it's another thing to be deceptive. I finished my drink and left. Two days later she sent me an online greeting with a dozen red roses. I deleted the file and never replied.

Listen up people, CHECK THOSE NUMBERS. There is nothing wrong with just knowing right from the start if the person you will be dating at least lives in the town that they say they do.

Another major tool in the player's toolbox besides the cell phone is the beeper or personal pager. If your prospective date cannot at least give you a real phone number, then they should not be treated as a real person either. It is far too easy to leave cell phone numbers with the excuse that you cannot reach the player otherwise. If that's what they are saying, I'd think twice.

In today's world of rapid and convenient communications, it is still essential to have some pretty solid bases in which you can contact people. One thing we learned right after the 9-11 disaster was that cell phones are not entirely reliable. There was almost no cell phone service for nearly three days following the disaster. Regular phone service was, however, very reliable and working within hours. If the only number a person can give you is a cell phone number, all I am saying is put up a red flag. Become very skeptical of anyone who is impossible to reach. Your first thought should be that they are a player, or even worse, married.

Another weapon in the arsenal of communications technology is the answering services or answering machines. It is far too easy to ask your bachelor friend or sympathetic relative if you can keep a spare phone line in their house or apartment and check your messages from a distance. If you notice that every time you call your prospective mate you get a call back from other numbers, it may very well be the case. It is a little more difficult if they have a telephone system answering service, then of course you are constantly talking into a phone that may never ring at home. It could very well be that he or she has told their spouse that they need a computer line—no one really knows that it also serves as a silent messenger for incoming calls as well.

Of course, some of the more sophisticated players can be using rental cars to not only keep you guessing, also impress you. Usually rentals have at least some small sticker on them somewhere; it's always prudent to pry by looking in the glove compartment. Does it look as if your date uses this car all the time? Spare change in the ashtray is a clue!

Some players actually still use one of the oldest tricks in the book, and that is using a pay phone. Many pay phones in New Jersey after the three-digit exchange start with the numbers 97XX, 98XX or 99XX. I am not sure if that is the case all over, but it is generally true here.

One of the best things to come along in decades for players of all types is the phone card. You can actually call from the convenience of your own home, and using the access number on the phone card, block YOUR number from coming up on THEIR caller ID. Another advantage that it is being used for was to prevent the player's wife or husband from spotting toll calls on the local phone bill. For every system, there is an anti-system.

One of the very best devices that has been a windfall to the telephone company is caller ID. Unfortunately, there are so many options that can be used to defeat it that now it has become a game. I happen to have call block on my phone, which means people who try to block the number can't get through. It is almost useless because anyone can call from a pay phone and still remain anonymous. There is no tracking the millions of phone cards in use today. Calling from ANY phone anywhere and using the phone card access number completely thwarts the call block option.

So what's the point? Insist on real information, ask the right questions, and get their home, work and cell numbers. Ask for addresses, especially if you are a woman and going to meet a man. Almost all men should know their license plate number—don't be embarrassed ASK FOR IT! Before you go on a date, give all that information to your best friend. You never know if it might be needed.

Police Notes—Chapter Nine, Tools of the Trade:

1. Information is the single best tool that you can use to make determinations about Internet dating and romance. Get as much information as possible.

2. Anonymous screen names are great tools to hide or disguise yourself when first meeting someone. Just remember that they can do the same.

3. Cell Phones come up on Caller Id, but not all the time. Those numbers can usually be traced back to a credit card, although now you can get pay as you go cellular service, which is virtually undetectable.

4. Be aware that some people have pagers with voice mail. If you never get a person on the phone, but rely exclusively on call-backs, the odds are good that you are calling a pager/voice mail service.

5. Cell phones are becoming more and more commonplace. Some people actually are using them now instead of line phones as their regular phone. I would be cautious, though, of anyone who did not have any other phone number except a cell number to give you.

6. Line answering services, such that you might contract with your phone company, can effectively screen your calls. They can also be used by players to screen their calls, possibly so that their husband or wife won't know they are having an affair. Make a note of what number you call, and if the person you are interested in answers the phone at that number.

7. Calling information (411) to cross-check the three digit telephone exchange with the city or town that your online mate has given you as their address is always a good, quick honesty check.

Intuition

This subject in particular has been playing through my mind since I first conceived the idea of this book. Having been involved in police work for twenty-five years, and just being naturally curious, this concept more than any I can testify has been "field tested." In my line of work, intuition can literally mean the difference between life and death. Being a policeman, you begin to develop that sense, call it anticipation or just call it for what it is, your "gut" talking to you. The decisions you make based on feeling rather than facts are almost universally correct. I have, through the years in police work, crisis counseling and off the job through my own interests, pursued a life's study of behavioral science. It was always my passion to understand just what it was that drove people to do the things that they do.

I'm not only talking about criminals here—I'm also talking about those of us who put our own lives on the line time and time again. I have, along with my colleagues, run into burning buildings to get people out, crashed through doors countless times wondering each and every time if there was a person with a loaded gun just waiting on the other side. We have risked life and limb in any number of ways—always without thought, working only with our own "gut" feelings.

Of course on the other side of the spectrum, there is a question that I have always had in my mind. What drives people to risk their own lives, liberties, careers and families to do the things they do, that are criminal or deceptive? Not only through stealing and taking property that belongs to another, but what pain and suffering they inflict on another human being has always been a question to many of us who wear a blue uniform every day. In many of those cases, passion is a driving force. Whether it is a passion to possess, manifesting itself in the form of greed, or a passion to control, manifesting itself in the form of anger, we are all victims of this misguided passion, which sometimes disguises itself as loyalty, interest, generosity or even love. What tool can we employ to guard against the camouflage of such noble virtues? The answer, of course, is intuition.

Fairly recently I can think of an instance in which I met a woman, Ginger. She was probably the most innocent looking person you could ever imagine. Of course as in all relationships, she had her good qualities and her baggage, as many of us do—it's all part and parcel of the whole dating relationship. We all have those good points and bad, they actually turn out to be the things that comprise the unspoken mental checklist that we use to size each other up.

In this particular case we did everything right…we met at a restaurant for the first date, and then called each other and planned another. So, on the second date, we decided that we would watch some sports on my big screen TV, kick back and order in some steamed Alaskan king crab claws, clams and shrimp. It would be the big screen sports coupled with a seafood feast and a couple of cold beers. All in all it was completely relaxed and we were having a great time…not just an ok time, or even a good time, we were having a *great* time. Everything seemed to be going better than we could have ever expected. It was somewhere around the seventh inning stretch that we decided to kiss each other and that was going even better than I would have imagined. All of a sudden she jumped up and said, "OK where's the cameras?" Needless to say I said, "What? What are you talking about?" She then went on to a rant about knowing that I was going to videotape what we were doing so that I could show it to my "cop friends." Well, I calmed her down and I assured her that there were no cameras, and that if she just wanted to sit calmly and watch the game that would be fine. Well, she did calm down and we resumed getting comfortable with each other. Here is where I made my BIG mistake. My intuition was kicking in…it was screaming at me ABORT! ABORT! ABORT! But I didn't listen. I thought she was too nice and just needed some time. Throughout this short-lived relationship, my intuition had been screaming, "DANGER WILL ROBINSON! DANGER!" But I didn't listen. Do you know why? Well let's just say that my cop ego had probably pushed the OVERRIDE button and I thought I knew better. Ginger turned out to be a nightmare. It was problem after problem—and in the end, I was beginning to question if it was me. That's FINALLY when the red flags went up. I knew that I was really stable and had good common sense. The problem was that I kept looking for the best in her—as I had done with many people before. There was no redeeming quality. It turned out that she was, in fact, a self-destructive co-dependent that in the end returned back to her ex-husband who had beaten her senseless in the past! It was difficult for me emotionally, and it didn't have to be, all the warning signs were there. I just decided not to listen to them.

Listen up people, if it can happen to me, it can happen to you! Don't ever let your emotion rule your own reason. Trust your GUT reaction and make conscious decisions.

Here is a technique that has proven itself time and time again. If those red flags go up, share with your mother, father, sister or brother, pick a good friend, but get someone, ANYONE who can step away from the situation and give you good advice. Ginger was, for me, an accident waiting to happen. In the end the mental image that finally allowed me to break free emotionally was that I had to imagine her standing next to me with a hand grenade. I saw her pull the pin. My next decision was how close did I want to be when that thing goes off?! That image allowed me to take flight and never look back.

Another sad story that I had learned of in a recent interview involved a man who met the woman of his dreams online. He dated her, and of course now in retrospect he says that the flags were there all the time. The way he categorizes the relationship to me was by saying, "She was a hottie." I can only think those emotions kicked his testosterone level into overdrive. He also was drowning in a sea of emotion and had no life preserver. He did have his intuition. However, he didn't have anyone to help him with his intuitive feelings. He needed someone to help him compare them with his emotional feelings. People, I CANNOT SAY THIS ENOUGH. You must always trust your intuition.

He owned some apartments and he offered to give her an apartment to stay in. As he tells his story, he continues to pepper the conversation with all kinds of references that he should have listened to. He keeps saying he "should have known better, all the signs were there." Well, over the course of a month or so his new love had moved into the apartment with at least a dozen of her motorcycle gang friends. The other apartment tenants were then raising all kinds of issues and started withholding rent. As he was about to begin eviction proceedings so that he can divorce himself from this self-created nightmare, she got her lawyer to serve him with papers of her own, a paternity suit. She announced that she was now pregnant with his child. The story continues that eventually he worked through all this and at the same time he sued to obtain custody of his now unplanned newborn child. The mother disappeared. All of this could have been avoided if he would have only listened to his inner self warning him.

Intuition, I tell people all the time, is your single greatest defense against getting caught up in a situation that you'd rather not be in. I'd rather not get into a discussion of whether there are psychic forces at work or anything that has to do with a sixth sense. I would much rather think that through your own years of experience, you have acquired the basic knowledge that you developed for your own self-defense. Knowledge of body language, language, voice and tonal inflections and communications are all part of your life skills. When listening to people and watching them, you pick up on very subtle clues that trigger within your mind the red flags that alert you to danger. If you are consciously aware of these red flags, and you act on them, you can and will be able to emerge virtually unscathed. It always seems to amaze me how people will discount these inner feelings. On the other hand, the same people always seem to recognize that the signs were always there all along. They just made a conscious decision to act against their own self-interest.

Because of the fact that everyone has this ability, and that they can actually act on it, it is more than obvious that we should seize upon this ability to protect ourselves. The best technique is to separate our internal emotions from our internal senses. Sometimes they work contradictory to each other and that is usually because our egos get into the mix. We either have a sense of self-worth and feel we deserve to have a certain special someone in our lives, or we fool ourselves into thinking that we cannot possibly be making these bad choices.

The facts are simple; there are bad people out there. In my case, Ginger was just plain bad. She was self-destructive and coupled with her own twisted set of personal values and issues, she took advantage of my kindly nature. But it would be unfair to place all the blame on her because, once again, I along with everyone else can join in the chorus and say, "the signs were there." But in many cases, you may find that the people who enter your life are not necessarily bad, just bad for you. On the other hand, some people are just plain deceitful. So we have a wide spectrum of people whom we will be meeting on the Internet that may, in fact, be perfect for us. On the other hand, they may be bad for us and may be psychologically or emotionally damaged. In the worst cases they could quite possibly be extremely evil in the sense that they are exploitive, violent or dangerous.

So without beating this to death, I must once again tell you that the technique is to share your feelings and your intuitive senses with another more objective person. This will allow you to get outside of yourself and see things through the eyes of someone you trust. No one likes to throw away an investment they have made in a relationship. After several months or more, you may become mired down and can't see the forest from the trees. In many of those cases even listening to those around you becomes difficult because you have already started to get settled into the pattern or comfort zone that comes along with the relationship. The trick here is to use your own intuition right from the start as an early warning system.

I met another girl online and we exchanged a few e-mails and of course chatted online. After a short time, we exchanged phone numbers and when we talked there were all kinds of red flags popping up. Some of the "issues" that she raised was that she didn't like children, (I have two), another was that she seemed to like to go out drinking and partying, (I don't drink) and lastly, she seemed like she was still more interested in casual dating, whereas I was looking for a more long-term relationship.

I was now aware of our incompatibility, and immediately switched from my emotional mind to my logical mind. Everything became rapidly crystal clear to me, and I believe to her as well. After about perhaps fifteen minutes more of conversation I (rather proudly) said, "I just don't think we would be compatible." I hung up the phone and tossed her phone number into the trash can.

In the past I might have thought that I should get to know her better. I might have met her to see how we worked in person. That is simply a waste of her time as well as mine. It wouldn't have mattered if she looked like a runway model and drove up in a hundred thousand dollar car, none of it mattered because no matter what was on the outside, inside she wasn't right for me.

The signs were there, except in this case I recognized them beforehand and not in retrospect. Now when I get a minute or two, I replay our phone conversation by talking about it with my trusted advisor and best friend; my cousin Mark. The reason I do this is so that I more firmly implant in my own conscious mind those warning signs. I do that so that I can recognize them in the future even more quickly. Reinforce within yourself just what you are willing to accept and what immediately you think will disqualify a date from becoming a relationship. I believe that when two people meet who are compatible, if they are honest with each other they can work through differences. The sign of a truly mature person is their own ability to accept themselves for who and what they are.

Anyone who enters your life should bring with them honesty, loyalty and friendship. After those three basics are firmly planted within the foundation of a relationship anything is possible. If any of them are deficient, your onboard senses should detect that, and you should begin to notice the warning signs early on, before you are emotionally committed.

Intuition is real. You have seen it work in the animal kingdom where it is widely recognized as instincts. Animals use it for self-defense. Humans possess the same ability, for the same reason. It sometimes comes across as a cold feeling or as a chill, or sometimes it comes across as a warm feeling, a very uncomfortable sweat. Clammy hands, nervousness, an uncomfortable feeling and restlessness are all ways that your body is telling you that something isn't right. It is ok to be a little nervous or shy when first meeting someone, but be aware of the difference. If you should learn anything, you should learn that your intuition doesn't lie—and that if it could happen to me, it could happen to you.

In my case, I lost some time and a little emotional investment. In time I will forget it ever happened and I won't even classify the experience as a bad memory. In the case of the man I interviewed with the apartments, he will have a reminder with him for the rest of his life.

Listen up once again people; your intuition is the best device you have with regards to dating safety. It never fails, and it is always on. Recognize the early warning signs and please act on them. If you are in doubt at all, remember the technique of calling up someone and getting their advice. Between your own "gut" feelings and the input from a trusted advisor, you cannot go wrong. My prime advice in all of this is to act fast. The sooner you do, the less you will have to pay. And last but not least, if the relationship is good and the person is sincere, you won't have to use any of this. There are good people out there too. I just don't have to warn you about them!

Police Notes—Chapter Ten, Intuition:

1. Intuition sometimes means just following your "gut reaction."
2. Most of the time that first impression, or your instinct, is the most accurate assessment you can make.
3. More than anything else, it will be your intuition that brings to your minds attention the red flags that something is not right in any situation.
4. You must be cautious, because although intuition is very powerful, it is also very subtle. It can easily be put on hold if your emotions are running very high.
5. The best choices you can make in situations and relationships involves a combination of intuition and logic. Keep emotions out of the equation.
6. Intuition has been seen in the animal kingdom as instincts. It works, and can mean the difference between life and death. It is important to learn how to trust your intuition.

Tricks of the Trade

The online players have to be able to keep weaving and dodging in order to keep in the "play" of the "game". I have been victimized by some of this, and admittedly, I have played in some of it. Let's start with some basic assumptions. If you are interested in a relationship, these words should not even enter into your vocabulary. There should be no "play"; there should be no "games" there should be honesty, loyalty and friendship, all for starters.

One thing that took me a long, long time to learn was what I call rule number one in the gamesmanship of being a player. The first thing that all players state unequivocally is that *they are not into games*. That is a hard, fast and solid rule. Would you ever consider it odd to sit with someone and have him or her exclaim, "I'm not a murderer?" Wouldn't it be a little unusual to be having either a phone conversation with someone or sitting across with them from dinner and they blurt out, "I never stole anything?" Of course, red flags would go up all over the place. In my experience, the best camouflage ever perpetrated on me was when my dates would say they weren't players, they weren't into games or they didn't like people who played games. Now when I hear that, rule number one comes to mind, Ah-ha, I'm with a player!

I know that's not all that much of a trick, but it is something worth mentioning. In fact, it opens up the door to just that subject, listening. The best trick of the trade that you can use is to listen and keep notes. If you were interested in buying a new car, you'd go around, price compare and jot down some notes. The same holds true when you are shopping for your friends around the holidays. You might get ideas of who likes what. And, after some careful deliberation, you might buy that car. You may even get that polka dot tie for your boss. When you are Internet shopping for a new partner, you should be just as involved in the process.

I think it's important for me to say here that of course you wouldn't have to do any of this if you are just fooling around, playing or toying with people. I'm addressing this chapter as well as this whole book to people who are serious about finding a real romance through the Internet, personals or dating services.

One of the best tricks of the trade is to check out your online partner as best as you can. In the initial phases of "meeting" someone online there are a few basics that everyone should do almost automatically.

In America Online and in most other services as well, there is space provided for the member to list some kind of description of themselves. This is known in most of the services as the member's directory. It usually has some cursory information about the person. Here's what I consider important: if a man or a woman wants to seriously meet someone online, they should be aware that the person that they are going to approach might be concerned. One of the best ways to alleviate that concern is to have at least sufficient information in the member's directory to demonstrate that you are credible. There's nothing wrong with a prospective date knowing your first name, your age or date of birth, and the town and state you live in. Listing a few hobbies and interests along with a favorite quote can add real character to the person who owns the screen name they are seeing. Of course, by now we all recognize that this can be a whole online phony persona. But putting that aside, and for this moment assuming that both parties are sincere, those basics should be required.

After a few initial e-mails, it is not unreasonable to ask for a photo. There is nothing wrong with wanting to put a face onto the personality that is rapidly developing. If the person is within maybe ten or fifteen miles away, that's about a half-hour drive by car. It is not a major road trip. If you meet each other blind for coffee and it doesn't work, you still have time to go home and cut the lawn. If, on the other hand, you were corresponding with someone that potentially may ask you to put aside a major portion of time, which could be fifty to seventy five miles away, I'd ask for the pic. Remember people; no pic, no date, simple! If you are concerned with safety, I'd think it would be more than reasonable to ask for the pic. You print out two copies and give one to a friend. If the person who shows up is not the person in the picture, you should politely say, "I'm sorry you must have me mistaken for someone else," and GET OUT OF THERE!

So, how about this person online? What do you know about them? On America Online, you have the ability to log on with seven different screen names. Once you have e-mailed a few times and perhaps chatted, you can log on under another name and click "locate" to find where your new-found love is on the system. Would you be surprised if this big husky guy who you thought was your own true love was hanging around in a chat room called " men who flirt" or, what if he was in a chat room called " men who flirt…with other men". It's an interesting way for you to find out what your partner is doing when they think you are not online.

One of the low down, meanest and dirtiest tricks in the book is to start an online relationship with someone and learn all about them. After a bunch of e-mails, a dozen or so instant messages and conceivably even actual dating, you have a pretty good feeling for what this person is all about. Of course, at that point you can "construct" an online portrait or profile of just what they like. Now, acting under an assumed new identity you can flirt with them or tease them or actually hit on them for a date, as another person online. If your partner is loyal to only you, you will know in a minute. If, however, he or she "takes the bait" and asks for your phone number, you know that you have been getting perhaps a little too close to a "player."

I am not in favor of some of the more underhanded methods of checking on people because they actually, in my own judgment, are an invasion of privacy. I have heard of people doing this to others, so I make mention of the fact that I know it's done. One person I know had promised to install some "new software" on his girlfriend's computer and while doing that downloaded her entire download directory so he could see who she was corresponding with and what was being sent to her. Another computer super sleuth, this time a female, had convinced her boyfriend that she had her America Online Service shut off because of a "credit card problem." She claimed that she had to do some serious research for a college project. She asked for his password and began logging on as him when he was at work. She said it was, "just to see what would happen."

It is prudent and wise to check on online personalities. Like everything else, though, balance and good judgment must be the measure. If a potential date has fudged a little on their birthday, well, let's face it, we all have egos. Someone else may trim off their weight or forget that their hair color isn't actually brown, it's more like gray-brown! There is something to be said about genuine shyness, a little embarrassment and just plain innocence. Everyone online is not a crook, a con or a gypsy. It's good to go in with a certain caution, but we cannot become paranoid either. One girl I met said her attitude about the men she met before venturing on the Internet was a simple metaphor, "Men are like parking spaces, all the good one's are taken, and the only one's left are handicapped!" She had better results online!

There are a number of services out there that will help you. These services change rapidly, so I'm not going to mention any of them by name. They specialize in checking out people for you. Of course, there is a charge involved. It all depends on how much you want to spend and how much you want to know. You can do some basic checking yourself. There are ways to find someone on the Internet and check to see if that person has placed any messages on any one of the thousands of public access bulletin boards still being used throughout the system. It would be worth your while if you really think you like someone, to do that yourself or ask one of your computer guru friends to help. I think as a potential partner you would want to know that the nice person you really were taking a liking to is all over the Internet recruiting for a subversive organization.

Location, location, location! That alone is what gives us a sense of permanence and with that, some degree of security. You can understand that some people, a very small portion of our society, is totally transient. Even people in military professions do not change duty assignments every few months. I had the occasion to meet a girl online who happened to pose a serious dilemma to me. Living here in New Jersey, she was geographically convenient in Manhattan. The problem was that she was living on the Upper West Side. Her apartment was on the thirtieth floor. Now I knew that sounds pretty good, but how was I to know. She could have been living in a public housing shelter. She also could have easily been going online at the public library, all the while playing me, for all I knew. At this point I was being cautious. She did leave me a phone number and we called each other. She was usually not available most of the time. I wanted to know if she was for real. I also wanted to see if the address she gave was where she lived. I was stumped. Then I got the idea of the century. I simply called 1-800-Flowers (on the Internet 1-800-Flowers.com). I asked for the least expensive bouquet they could send which was around twenty-five dollars. I sent them to her with a note:

It was so nice talking with you on the phone, and I have been dying to meet you. Since this was our one-month anniversary, I thought I'd send these to tell you thank you for being so nice. Dennis

One of several things could have happened. I called about eight hours later to verify the delivery. Just like a check, if she didn't live there, the delivery would have bounced. Also, if for some reason her husband got the flowers, I'm sure I would have known about it just as fast. What had actually happened was the best-case scenario; she called me and thanked me. We are still friends to this day. It never turned out to be a love connection, but the investment paid off in friendship. As I figured it, just driving into Manhattan would have cost just as much. Between the gas, tolls and parking, I got away cheap. Even if I did drive there and I asked the doorman if she lived there, he probably would have told her. She could have been concerned as to what I was doing there asking about her. Saying it with flowers was the cheapest and best way to verify the address.

Asking about the cars that people drive can tell you a little something too. You can usually get a picture in your mind of how truthful a person is if they give you an overall picture of what they are all about. A person who claims to be in the six-figure category driving a 1978 Chevrolet might not be giving you the total picture. Along with cars, drivers license information, accidents, tickets, things like that may make you think twice about meeting this person and giving a real hard thought about allowing them into your life.

If you are seriously thinking about taking on a relationship with the man or woman of your dreams, you can ask some of the online services to check public documents about them. Learning that they have been married four times and never divorced should send up the red flags. Small things like bankruptcies, criminal arrests and active warrants can be a real eye opener if it pops up in a public records search. As I said earlier, there are a number of services that do those things for a fee, sometimes it is well worth it to make the small investment in the beginning to save you from the heartbreak later on. In some cases, getting your heart broken might be the least of your problems.

On the other hand, you must also be cautious about giving too much information out about yourself until you know with whom you are talking. I interviewed a man who had become involved in an interstate romance. They had gone back and forth in a stream of torrid e-mail for several weeks. She finally caught up with him in chat and according to him "was in a panic". She wanted to leave her husband and he was apparently very abusive. She claimed to be very afraid that her husband would find the e-mails, so she said she would meet him in chat every day when the husband was at work. After about two weeks, she asked for his number and they talked on the phone. The very next day she called again "in a panic", and said her husband destroyed her computer and that the only way they could continue was to talk on the phone. The man that I interviewed was very distraught when telling this story. He continued on that he was encouraging her to leave and that the phone calls gave him a real sense of purpose. She often said, "It was a miracle that you came into my life." She also courted him by saying he was her "knight in shining armor." She told him that her husband would check the phone bill so she needed a credit card to be able to call him, without it showing up on her phone bill. Mr. White Knight knew that the noble thing to do was to pick up the phone charges and readily allowed her to use his Visa Card by giving her the card number and expiration date. That was the last call he ever got from her. His credit card charges ran up to the three thousand-dollar limit and he had no way of even knowing who or where she was. She had been calling him and the number she gave him came back to a phone booth in Pittsburgh.

Two of my favorite tricks that I think work are simply knowing where and when to call. After we make phone contact I ask for the work number, even if you just call once to verify that Mr. or Mrs. Smith works there. That is a good credibility check. The other is the ability to call home anytime. I always ask how late can I call. I feel best when a prospective date says call me whenever you feel like it. I went out with my friends once and came home so pumped. The girl I was seeing was going to spend the evening at home. I called her just after midnight to tell her how the night went. She was so happy to hear from me. It made me feel so good to be able to call her. If someone poses unreasonable restrictions on your available calling time, that is usually a red flag.

Listen up people, for the last time here. A relationship should always start with honesty, loyalty and friendship. If for any reason any one of those three elements are missing, someone is fooling someone. Either a player is fooling you, or in some cases you are fooling yourself. There is no compromise on these three requirements. Everything else that comes along must be built up from them. If you start off short, you end up short.

Understanding that there are players out there who think that your emotions are theirs to be had are part and parcel of their game and can be a very hurtful reality. It becomes especially painful when you realize that a trust was given and was broken by them, someone whom you trusted. When you give something as important as that part of yourself, you stand there before them in extreme vulnerability. If you are in the relationship for any length of time, your mind can go into a tailspin thinking of what other things they could have done with your trust. Don't be blindsided by being careless. Be honest, be loyal and be a friend, but at the same time be careful.

There are many different ways of finding things out about the person you are interested in, as you have read. However, sometimes you may find yourself becoming a little more than just interested in a person. You may begin to find that your simple interest is beginning to take that fateful turn into involvement. As I had been indicating throughout this entire book, there is certainly something to be said about trusting your "gut reactions," your intuition. You have your first two lines of defense working for you if you only step back for a moment and listen to both your head and your gut. Sometimes, however, right in the middle of those two main defense batteries, the heart seems to get in the way. Because there is a need for professional assistance, I have had personal contact with a service called DateSmart.com. The people who run it are the best on the Internet at what they do. They do an assortment of background checks and they are dedicated to safe, personal relationships. Their motto is, "if you date…investigate." When you visit the DateSmart.com website there are dozens of testimonials and other horror stories about people who should have taken the precautions that we talk about here in this book. At the DateSmart.com website you can look through many more interesting testimonials as well as a wealth of other information.

I have dedicated my life to protecting people and that is why I had found it necessary to commit to writing the suggestions that I have put into this book. Also, I was hoping that the stories you have read along with the following case studies would leave an impression upon you to cause you to use logic when meeting people on the net. When your observations or intuition warn you that you need to "know more," the small price that you invest in DateSmart.com's service is money well spent.

On their web site they have a list of RED FLAGS that is excellent and I thought would be most helpful to include here. When you visit their site, you can click on any one of these flags and get more information about what to look for. In addition to that information, there are stories about them. The owner of the site, Carmen, is committed to giving the best possible service to her clients. She shares with me the desire to help people find truth and happiness on the Internet, but at the same time, strive for them to have every safety consideration and the ability to have the information they need that is accurate and up to date.

If you use good common sense, coupled with the opinions and observations of your friends, and if you take the time to keep a few notes, you will be well on your way to safety. You must also keep your emotions under control in order to get a good sense if the person you have met is everything they claim to be. If there is any question in your mind, or if your friends give you some feedback that sounds like you aren't thinking clearly, it would be worth your while to make a small investment in DateSmart.com. Dating services charge thousands to find the perfect mate. Consider conducting your own background check on your own prospective mate for a fraction of the cost. Before you become involved with someone, get involved in the process and make responsible decisions. Here is the list of RED FLAGS from the DateSmart.com web site:

1. *Does it seem too good to be true?*
2. *Is there something you can't quite put your finger on?*
3. *Are they secretive or elusive regarding their past?*
4. *Do they blame others for their problems?*
5. *Have they given you expensive gifts early in the relationship?*
6. *Have they asked you for money or use of credit cards?*
7. *Are they adamant about particular thoughts, beliefs or ideas?*
8. *Have they told you their parents or "ex" are deceased?*

9. *Have they told you they are in the CIA, FBI or other "secret Government Agency?*
10. *Do you have questions concerning the true identity of this person?*
11. *Have they blamed their ex-spouse for ruining their credit, their loss of home or property, their business or children?*

If any of these questions have come to your mind, or have been posed to you by close family or friends, the answers may be something you need to know. If you are involved with a person where they are entering your life (or are already in your life), you need this information to make judgments regarding the direction your own life is going.

To be able to chart your own course and feel safe, you need to get accurate information and get on with planning your future. A relationship, by its very nature, should be started with honesty, loyalty and friendship. If you have questions about these issues because your mate has been elusive or evasive, DateSmart.com is the best place to get peace of mind. If you do not have a computer, you can still access DateSmart.com by calling them toll free at: 1-888-84-CHECK.

Police Notes—Chapter Eleven, Tricks of the Trade:

1. *If you are truly interested in a relationship, game playing should not be part of it. It should be based on honesty, loyalty and friendship.*

2. *Whenever someone is going to enter into the game playing mode, they often start out by saying they are not into games. That can be very disarming to someone who doesn't expect it.*

3. *Listen and take notes. In chat, telephone conversations, or even after a date, it's a good idea to jot down a few important pieces of information, statements that your date made that you may want to verify later.*

4. *Always try to see what information your potential partner has already placed out there by reviewing any personal ads or listings in the member's directory.*

5. *Always ask for a photo. There is no better way to determine if a potential future mate is at least basically honest when you first meet them than by comparing them to their photo.*

6. *If your online mate sent a photo that was concealing or critically out of date, that should be a warning sign.*

7. *You can check out the person you're interested in using a different screen name. You can then go into the same chat rooms and follow the dialog that this person is engaged in.*

8. *If you are unsure if your already established relationship is secure, you can, under an assumed screen name, flirt with them or even try to set up a date.*

9. *It is always a good idea to send a card or something inexpensive in the mail to verify an actual address.*

10. *There are many online information banks and search services that can partially identify elements of the person you are interested in.*

11. *Never, never give out your credit card information to someone you met on the Internet.*

12. *If you are seriously interested in someone, and you want to check them out thoroughly, call: 1-888-84-CHECK or DateSmart.Com on the Internet.*

The Folders/Case Studies in
Internet Relationships

As I became a member of the cyber community, I was going through some incredible personal tragedy in my life. I lost my sister-in-law to cancer; several months later, I lost my oldest sister due to brain tumors, and within months my own mother died of cancer. During all of this, my police career was winding down and winding out. There were incredible political battles in my community, and being at the helm as the Chief of Operations was an incredibly stressful task. In all of this, my wife and I were being torn apart by all the pressures of family, career and personal issues, and became separated and eventually divorced.

Part of what kept me sane through it all, and helped to provide a safe and effective retreat, was my frequent visits to the cyber-world. In the beginning, I was pretty vulnerable. I was naive, even though I was a career police officer. I had my shortcoming and wasn't naturally distrusting. To get right to the point, I was played. I met people online who recognized immediately that I was in trouble emotionally—some wanted to latch onto me; others wanted to exploit me. Not that they were calculating or malicious, but they wanted THEIR needs fulfilled and I was convenient. I sure learned my lessons fast though. It didn't seem fast at the time.

It took about a year, but after awhile, I became wise to the players on the Internet and started to adapt. In time, I too became a player. I admit it—I was mad, hurt, and angry, and I wanted to go out and take some of what had been taken from me. That didn't last long though. I couldn't live with myself. I couldn't look into the mirror and accept the person that I was becoming. I thought, "God, why can't people just be honest?" But I wasn't being honest either. It seemed to me that loyalty was a fleeting thing. It also seemed that friendships were hard earned. But I persisted, and this book was born from all of that. I founded the principal of honesty, loyalty and friendship in all of my contacts, and I tried to inspire those with whom I had contact with to do the same. When I became real, the friendships also became real.

As my player days moved from the played through to the player, and out until I could become the man that I wanted to be, I amassed an incredible amount of research data. I saved so much of all my contacts with people, and that too helped me understand the change that was taking place in my life. I put all of the hard copy into folders. E-mails, chat logs, photos, personal notes, electronic cards—everything fit into several boxes the size of storage containers. This is the story of those folders and how they came about, and the people whom they represent. This is the reality of what was going on in the mind of this player. It might give you some insight or enjoyment, entertainment or amusement. I hope it helps you to understand. I hope it causes you to think.

Working with the Folders
Case Studies in Internet Dating

I'm sitting here in front of my computer. There are folders strewn all around me. They contain computer profiles, chat logs, e-mails and notes of all the people that I've met online.

As mentioned in previous chapters it is important to keep print outs of ads, photos, instant message logs and emails. Keeping poor notes can result in the following: You happen to meet a girl named SEXYLADY online, but because you are careless when you download her Pic (Photo) you accidentally misfile it as SHYONE. Then comes the day when you finally go to meet her. It is at that exact moment you remember that SEXYLADY wasn't really SEXY at all. Now you are really stuck. You have to make some quick decisions. So you immediately cancel the quiet little booth in the dark corner. Of course, what you thought was going to be the dream date owing to the picture confusion, has now turned into the "date from hell."

Again your memory haunts you when you look at your scribbled notes on the back of the wrongly printed photo and with that you have now resolved to get a better filing system.

Case Study Number One
Name: Susan
Screen Name: DragonFire
Location: California

Susan and I met as a result of her searching through the member directory. We had some common interests in metaphysics and things like remote viewing and other esoteric subjects. She had contacted me purely to work with a program that I was developing to find missing children and assist police in cases involving crimes where there were apparently no leads or clues. She and I became very close friends, more like business associates in the beginning. She was apparently a very gifted natural psychic and had worked with me on a few cases that were not in my hometown, but with other law enforcement agencies.

Eventually she gave me her phone number and we exchanged photos and became real compadres. After several months, she confided that she was in her thirties, but had been living with a man in his fifties. He was incredibly controlling and the computer was her only release.

As it turned out I became a real confidant to her and we started to take a liking to each other. The e-mails took on a noticeably personal tone, and after a few more contacts by phone we realized that we were connecting on a much more spiritual level. She had expressed a sincere desire to leave her partner, and I often teased her about how long the chain was on her radiator, and asked if she had enough chain to roam around the house.

There were many, many e-mails, instant message chats and phone calls. We really worked well together and she was an incredibly intuitive person. Her natural psychic ability allowed her to perceive my feeling across the continent. I was equally attuned to her, and I thought for sure that at some time in the future we would get to meet.

Sometime after several months, Susan just fell off. I never heard from her again. She deleted all of her screen names and her phone number was disconnected. There were a few other people who had been involved in the same "psychic network" that I worked with who I contacted and asked if they had heard from her. She had, in fact, just disappeared.

As I write this I can't help but wonder what ever happened to her. One of the problems with transcontinental relationships is exactly that, you never know, and it's almost impossible to find out. I probably have in my folder one hundred pieces of e-mail from Sue. She was a wonderful friend, and maybe if she reads this book, she will contact me. You look through the folders when this happens, for clues. It is always natural, at least for a moment, to think, "Was it something I could have prevented?" But after you use some logic and reason, you understand that it happens. After it happens a few times, you come to understand that some people just have to leave and their reasons are just that, their own reasons. It has nothing to do with you.

My best advice is that you never commit your heart until the person becomes real. It is unfair to all parties if too much emotional energy is invested in what actually amounts to a pen-pal relationship. It can and usually does lead to disappointment and heartache.

Case Study Number Two
Name: Deb
Screen Name: Karate Girl
Location: Manhattan, NY

Debbie was my first real online crush. Her original e-mail said:

Dear Dennis:
You sound wonderful…I would love to get to know you better…do you have a
photo as well? You and I have many similarities…and common interests. I look
forward to talking to you soon.
Deborah

At the time, her choice of the word wonderful was just what I needed. I had just moved out of the house and begun my separation. My mother was dying of cancer, and I just lost my sister. Deborah came into my life like a life preserver. I don't think there is any example that I could give that would better exemplify the actual POWER of Internet relationships like the friendship that was created between Debbie and I.

I was pretty much out on my own. I had just moved out and the only thing I had was a few articles of clothing, a few pieces of furniture and a whole big empty office space. I owned a small commercial office space and it was usually rented. As luck would have it, I didn't have it rented and decided to convert the space into a small apartment. I was a mess. I could never have met anyone, except for the fact that my computer allowed me to make contact. Deb was extremely supportive. I didn't get a chance to actually meet her in person for months. After she sent me the original e-mail, she sent a message that she was going off to Puerto Rico for a few weeks. Much to my surprise, she called me from Puerto Rico. In spite of the state of confusion and disorientation that I was in because of what was going on in my personal life, the call from Deb and the e-mails bolstered my spirits and provided for me more self-assurance than any counselor. I have to admit that she really came through for me.

I was looking forward to the couple weeks going by so that I could meet her in person. I sent her a stuffed Teddy Bear. She called back a few days later with some bad news. She said she would be staying in Puerto Rico another three to four weeks because she found a stray dog that she was nursing back to health. The bad news was that at the health ranch she was staying at there was a woman with terminal cancer. She gave the woman the Teddy Bear. I thought, "That's bad news?" She sounded saintly to me…I could only think, "Saving the stray dog, generous enough to give away your stuffed animal." Deb was really incredible.

I had originally wanted a romance. I can admit NOW, although I never would have back then—that I was on the rebound. OUCH, whenever you get separated that is probably the foulest word in the dictionary. The problem is that it comes across like some kind of silent plague. It seems that everyone around you knows that you have it except you. But I was rebounding and Deb and I had our share of ups and downs. So, about two months after the initial e-mail from her she got off the plane from Puerto Rico and we eventually met. Needless to say, the old Chemistry thing was not there, at least for romance. We had written each other so much, talked on the phone and had so many late night instant messaging sessions that we just HAD to be friends. Deb had walked me through one of the most difficult times of my life. I'd like to think that in it all I had walked beside her through my "dark night of the soul", and she was a capable guide and good friend.

To this day, Deb and I talk frequently. I'd have to say that we probably have some great conversation, compare notes and talk about goals and life's journey most of the time. Then we also probably have one good knock down, drag-em-down, fight/argument every couple or three months. Yeah, we have disagreements and arguments and all the stuff you would find in a "normal" friendship. But this one had its birth on the Internet. Anyone reading this who has become friends and confidants with an Internet person, will probably think that this is no big deal. But to someone who has not done so, it is possible to find friendship here.

Deb and I started out with Honesty, Loyalty and Friendship. What could have been one of the great romances of all time (In my mind only!) turned out to be one of the great friendships. The time you spend on the Internet meeting people never has to be considered a waste. You actually touch someone's life and interact with him or her in a way that can affect their own self-value and their own sense of purpose. You can, with your words, encourage them to do great things or discourage them from becoming depressed or despondent. You have the ability to reach across the planet and be "there" for them when no one else can be. In all Internet relationships, it is best to be a friend above all. In that investment that you make, you not only give a small part of yourself to someone else, you give yourself something too. The gift of friendship is a gift that returns to you, sometimes when you least expect it, but need it most.

Case Study Number Three
Name: Madonna
Screen Name: LeoBunny
Location: Essex County, NJ

Madonna was my first "real" relationship after I became separated. It was an absolutely incredible, almost miraculous, romance. I was actually cruising through the member's directory scanning for single females from New Jersey who happened to be online at two o'clock in the morning. There she was, LEOBUNNY…so I darted off to her a quick e-mail with my personal profile. I remember her saying, "Either this is a joke or this guy is something special." Well I did find her in the member's directory, and she admitted to having a liking for cops, so I was in.

As it turned out, she was a true LEO. She was a strong-willed woman, even though she was only twenty-eight years old. She described herself as having a striking look (which can go either way!), but she said she was attractive. She was five feet ten inches tall and well proportioned. So OK, I was hooked. We must have e-mailed back and forth playing games that first night twenty times. She FINALLY popped into my instant message window and said, "Let's cut the BS and chat already!" Well we chatted for about a half-hour before we exchanged numbers. She called me at about three thirty in the morning and we talked until seven.

We talked the next day and made a solid date. It was set for a couple of days away. Each night we were on the phone for at least five to six hours talking until the early morning hours. When we met for lunch, we were both exhausted. We were surprised that we really liked each other, but exhausted. I can honestly say that for both of us it was love at first sight.

Madonna and I really got along well. We saw each other about five nights a week, and we did a lot together. Of course, she had her issues and I had mine. We didn't really deal with them, though. I'd say we ignored them. That was eventually our undoing. In retrospect I was still coming off of the whole rebound thing. Madonna and I had some of the most fun times I have had dating. I'm honest enough now to say that we didn't have enough of them. She was absolutely wonderful. She was an extraordinary girlfriend, who after it was all over became an equally extraordinary friend to me.

Our relationship had its share of downs, but it was mostly ups. She was very, very proud of me and in her very own and unique LEO way, was extremely supportive. Her downside was that she had a temper. I could have easily dealt with that, I'd say ninety percent of the time it was just something she wanted to blow off steam about. All I had to do was back off. We were at different levels though. I learned much more about this later as I began to ease into the comfort zone of being separated and eventually divorced for a while.

She included me in her family and I did the same with her. We could have had a real romance. She absolutely cared for me. I was impatient, inexperienced and a little too unbending. It was new to me and I was trying to feel my way through this whole transformation. Just the same, she was a great girlfriend and remains a great friend.

We now follow each other through our personal careers, families and tragedies. I know whenever I have something in my life that really causes me to need someone, I can call her. She would be the first one in line to fight for me; I would do the same for her.

Case Study Number Four
Name: Sami
Screen Name: Sam1234
Location: North Jersey, NJ

Sami was certainly one of those people you meet and DO NOT forget. She was young, in her twenties, but she had been through a lot of life. Of course, I met her on the Internet. I answered her personal ad and we met. She was one of the very first girls that I met this way, and believe me, if she set the tone for Internet romance, there would have been none, and this book would not have been written.

One very interesting story about Sami: I dated her a few times, perhaps several times over a couple weeks. Then it didn't work, however, after a couple months we got back together and again, it didn't work. All along though, we kept in touch via e-mail and chat. Over the course of the year that we knew each other, she left me and started dating another guy. To show you what a small world this whole dimension of players is all about, as I was dating Madonna, Sami was dating Madonna's ex boyfriend. Well, things didn't work out so well between them and I later found out that Sami had a restraining order against him. That was not a good thing. Almost six months after that whole affair ended, I met a girl on line. Her name was Alexis. As I am sitting across the dinner table from her, she asks me if I knew other people from online. Of course I told her that I knew quite a few. She too, had been dating the same guy. Of all the thousands and thousands of people online, the circuit of players isn't all that large. You can make a reputation out there, good or bad.

I eventually lost track of Sami, but through it all I had come to know that people out there, as well as in the real world, cross paths. It is always better to leave as a friend, and wish them well. You never know whose lives they will touch with your memory.

Case Study Number Five
Name: SooLin
Screen Name: Soo1967
Location: Manhattan, NY

SooLin was one of those dates that really reminds you of a roller coaster. She had all the potential of being "the one". The problem is WHICH one, the perfect one, or the fatal attraction. She initially responded to my personal ad with:

Hi Dennis,
Read your ad tonight. You mentioned the inside person, but you didn't describe yourself. I feel the same as you do. Don't want to play games. Need someone who will be there 100% as I would. I am an American-Chinese. Born on the west coast of the United States and raised in the South. I relocated to New York about ten years ago. If you are interested in getting to know me, please e-mail me.
Soo

As it turned out, we exchanged phone numbers almost within a week of the first e-mail. Soo had caught me online a day or so after the e-mail, and we chatted for a few days. We agreed to meet in Manhattan. I met her there and the chemistry was off. It wasn't there, but yet there was potential. I decided to give it a shot. Soo and I talked on the phone regularly. I'd say we talked about three or four times a week. We dated about once a week. I would meet her in New York and we would hang around the city, or go to her apartment. She came to New Jersey a few times and we would do things here.

As the weeks went by, there was no spark in the relationship. She was trying her best to make things more intimate and bring us together, but it wasn't happening. I sensed that she wanted it to work. I also sensed that she wanted it to work for her more than for us. Soo needed someone in her life at that time. I would have liked that too. But I wasn't ready to be settling into a long-term relationship. I wasn't divorced yet, and I liked being able to see her occasionally, but not as often as I think she wanted to. I had some important career things going on in my life, and in the middle of it all I was working through finalizing the divorce.

It was at that time that she did something terrible. The two of us could have worked closer together given a reasonable time frame, and worked towards common goals, but she was getting impatient. For whatever reason, she was mistrusting and I didn't like that. She asked me several times about my whereabouts and she seemed to try and "trick" me. This set off alarm bells and that is one of the reasons that I chose to keep my distance. I was now feeling more self-confident. I had a few good relationships and dating experiences behind me. I was getting great support from the female friends I had made online. I didn't want to work in a situation where there was mistrust or lack of confidence. It was draining to be exposed to.

SooLin took it upon herself to have a girlfriend of hers flirt with me online, and she had the girlfriend literally badger me into conversation. Her girlfriend kept hitting on me in instant message and with a steady bombardment of e-mails. Eventually her girlfriend sent me her phone number and I called. Her girlfriend had done everything short of sending a cab to pick me up! We never met. I wasn't interested, nor did I have the time or patience for someone who was coming on so strong. SooLin started shooting very nasty e-mails to me, and exposed the ruse.

Needless to say, I was more than angry. It was, to me, a betrayal. Her girlfriend had purposely tried to bait me into a relationship, and had played out a melodrama that backfired for SooLin. What was once a very tame and gentle woman became a very nasty, self-centered and conniving person. I did not want her in my life, not as a girlfriend, and not even as a friend.

After I let her know that I did not want any kind of a relationship, she began a literal barrage of hate mail against me. She had taken our series of dates, and, in her mind, projected into them a relationship that was just not there. I was fully out of my own malaise by then and I had the ability to see things very clearly. On top of that, every decision I had been making was being done with input and feedback from my closest friends, both male and female. There was almost universal agreement that she was a fatal attraction.

She ended the relationship with a bunch of hollow threats in which she was going to write letters about me to my employer and the newspapers. She had alluded to the fact that I had misled her and used her. None of it was true. Fortunately for me, I had saved every e-mail she sent and printed out our chat logs. If I had to chronicle how the relationship progressed and how it had deteriorated, it was all right there, literally in black and white. She seemed like a very nice, quiet, innocent person in the beginning. At least it appeared that way from the outside. It's once you get inside of a person, and get to know what they are hiding within the interior portions of their personality, that you realize that what you see isn't always what you get.

I had shut her out of my e-mail, my instant message box and never answered the phone after that. In time she just disappeared. Thank God for privacy controls on the Internet.

Case Study Number Six
Name: Terri
Screen Name: Terri127
Location: Union County, NJ

Terri and I had met online. I had answered a personal ad that she had placed. There were some real problems right from the start. She was extremely suspicious and distrusting. She had placed an ad online and she said that she was ready to date, but she had the very, very annoying habit of questioning everything. She kept constantly trying to trip me up and had double-checked everything I said.

I met her at a sports event. She had been playing ball for her own home-town women's softball team. She was there with her daughter and she was nice. But she just kept asking the same questions over and over, and actually tried to get me to say the same answer differently. We had some phone conversations and it was more of the same.

I thought that if I gave it a little time things might work out if she felt more comfortable and took some time to get to know me. We went to a concert together, but I got the impression during the whole event that she just couldn't relax. I had begun to feel very anxious myself. I called her for another date, and met her one more time. Things had not progressed at all since the first time we met, and almost a month had gone by. I wasn't going to deal with a long-term trust issue. I didn't know if it could or would ever be resolved. She didn't seem to want to work on it. It seemed more like that was her protection, to keep on checking and not trusting. After the month of trying, I eventually ended the relationship.

Case Study Number Seven
Name: Liz
Screen Name: Liz517
Location: Middlesex County, NJ

This was the date that convinced me of several things. The first was No Picture, No Date. I was totally ambushed on this one, and the reason was simple. I had contacted her as a result of a personal ad that she posted at one of the pay services that I was browsing in. The attractive feature was that she was close by. She lived in the same county that I did. We exchanged e-mails back and forth for about two weeks. Liz was not a member of America Online, so we never got a chance to chat. It was extremely cumbersome writing back and forth, but after a while, it worked.

After the second week, we exchanged phone numbers and talked on the phone for about a week. We finally agreed to meet at my favorite restaurant (my big mistake). Everyone knew me there, and I showed up early thinking that Liz was going to be the "real deal". As I said previously, she said a LOT on the phone that had me anxious to meet her. I definitely got my first lesson in "sexual innuendo". Any woman who resorts to THAT tactic is always going to be substandard in my book. Of course, I didn't know that at the time, and that is why it is important enough to put into this book. Other than the lesson to be learned, this file should have been burned.

She peppered all of our conversations about how "good" she was and how "she knew her stuff" and made all kinds of statements that, quite honestly, threw my testosterone levels to record heights. When she walked in, I thought I would like to crawl under a table. All the people that knew me did a double take and just "backed off". My expectations didn't meet reality. They were totally deflated. It was a whole new experience to me and one that I will never forget.

In retrospect, I can see where I was at the time and being totally honest with myself, I thought that I had this break coming. There are no breaks that come, and wishing just doesn't make it. If a person talks like a pig on the phone, don't expect her to look like an angel when she walks through the door. It was a simple lesson. If it talks like a pig, walks like a pig, and acts like a pig, the odds are it will also *look* like a pig.

The reality of the situation is to just be careful what you ask for, because you just might get it. We had a drink and the date was over. Now that I've written this into the book, I can finally burn the file.

Case Study Number Eight
Name: Patty
Screen Name: PoohBear
Location: North Jersey, NJ

This was beyond a doubt the biggest eye opener for me as far as No Pic, No Date, and the fact that just because someone comes with "papers", it doesn't mean they have a pedigree.

Patty wrote to me as a result of her reading my personal ad somewhere in the system. She had actually been very adept at writing skills, and of course she should have been; she was a full college professor and her specialty was in early childhood development. I was extremely impressed with the credentials (my mistake) and I thought she would be my intellectual equal. I loved behavioral psychology, and I thought this would be an evening that I wouldn't forget (I was right about that!)

We exchanged e-mails for only a couple of days before we exchanged phone numbers. She was excited about meeting me, mainly because she said that she knew I was involved in law enforcement. Although she never said it—I am fairly sure she called the police station to see if I actually worked there. She seemed to be extremely cautious about giving up any personal information. I was somewhat aware that she was being highly guarded and red flags should have been going up all over the place. As it turned out, my intuition was absolutely correct. I had chosen not to trust my gut feeling because of two reasons. I thought her educational level would put her over the top, and I also thought that since she was an academic, she was probably just a little bit to the left politically and kind of liberal. I chalked it off as a right to privacy choice that she had made. I was wrong—it had nothing to do with privacy or choice. It had to do with emotional trauma and abject fear.

I arrived at the restaurant expecting to see this contemporary, stylish, educated and well-groomed college professor. Well let me say this, although she WAS a college professor, it ends there. She had on a full-length cloth coat that went from her neck to her ankles; She refused to take it off all during dinner. It was mid-March, and actually the restaurant was rather warm. She did not care. She wanted that suit of armor to protect her and sat at dinner with a coat on. As if that wasn't enough, her hair was absolutely not combed and not washed. It was the most oily, greasy, dirty hair I have ever seen. I could have almost sworn it was dripping from needing a shampoo. Her fingernails were long and dirty. Her entire attitude was that people either liked her for the "person" that she was or they didn't have to like her at all. She talked with food in her mouth and had no personal grooming habits and no manners whatsoever. She was both arrogant and unsophisticated.

I thought to myself, "Dennis, if you were blind, this might be meaningless to you, so let's at least pick her brains about Internet dating experiences." As I quizzed her about just that, she became somewhat irate. Apparently other men (more experienced) had walked out on her on other dates and some just flat out refused to even acknowledge her. To be completely on point here, she had NOTHING to offer.

I finished my meal and left. I was so totally overwhelmed by the fact that this person was involved in the field of psychology and at the same time was completely clueless as to her own psychological makeup that I was numb.

Of course, upon reading this, there are many lessons that I've learned here. There is no point in a recap. As I have said throughout this entire book, I've been a police officer for more than two decades; just when you think you've seen it all, well, something else comes along.

Case Study Number Nine
Name: Evie
Screen Name: Evie34
Location: Upstate New York

Evie and I were two soulmates in search of a relationship. The odds that the two of us would ever find each other were phenomenal. Fate had brought us together and it was fate that had kept us apart. If ever there was a mystical, magical story of two star-crossed lovers, it was Evie and I.

She had read one of my personal ads and as it turned out we had written back and forth to each other. For whatever reason, probably because I had found someone else, I had fallen out of contact with her for a couple of months. For the initial contact, we were like two ships passing each other in the night. The second time that we got together though, things were quite different. We hit it off on e-mail really, really well. It was only a short period of time before we caught up to each other in chat, and that didn't last very long. We almost immediately moved to the telephone and we pretty much exhausted each other almost every night. We were laughing together, crying together and really getting to know each other. The more we talked, the more phenomenal the whole story had became.

Evie and I started out just sharing fun stories, but it wasn't long before we started talking about things that were all about us. There were some incredible parallels in our lives that seemed to defy the odds that two people so far apart and from such different backgrounds could be so similar. She confided in me often, and we shared parts of ourselves with each other that no one else ever knew. It wasn't long before I decided that I was going to make the trip to Upstate New York and see her. We had already seen each other's pictures, and we thought things would be all right as far as the romance part of the relationship was concerned.

Well, the fateful day came and I was on my way. I checked into the hotel and I waited in the lounge. Evie walked in and it was instant REJECTION! So much for THAT idea. Things were extremely uncomfortable, for at least the first hour. Then the whole personality thing kicked in, and actually it was our two souls that began reaching out for each other. We couldn't have fought that attraction even if we tried. Evie came up to the hotel room and we began talking and laughing all over again, like we had on the phone. She spent the night, and we had probably one of the most intense bonding experiences ever. The next day we goofed around a lot, did some fun stuff and shared more of each other with each other. In the background, however, there was an undercurrent. We both felt it, we both knew it. The romance was not guaranteed, things were moving in a new direction. We felt the love, it was incredibly powerful stuff, but there was an overwhelming feeling of connectedness that seemed to crowd out the romance. Neither of us ever felt anything like that before.

In the weeks following my trip Upstate, we kept in touch and she came down to New Jersey. She spent time here with me and we kind of reconciled the fact that although we had our own lives, neither of us would be relocating. Evie moved further north in 1999 and we still keep in touch.

I never thought that I would include this story in this book. It didn't seem to have the "flavor" of all the others. The romance part certainly was not there, and there was no crazy or funny ending.

This was simply two people who met and became good friends.

Case Study Number Ten
Name: Fran
Screen Name: Woops
Location: Central New Jersey

This is an extremely funny story about some coincidences on the Internet. I met Fran when I responded to a personal ad that she posted. I was lucky to be able to get to meet her because when we did meet she said that the response to her ad had been so overwhelming that she had only posted it for a week and took it down.

Fran was younger; in her twenties, and I wasn't sure where this was going, but I was at the point where I was enjoying just getting out and meeting different people. We clicked in e-mail, never chatted, but went directly to the phone. As we began to compare notes and started talking to each other, it turned out that she had actually dated a close friend of my nephew. So we were already practically related, and we hadn't even met.

Fran and I knew even before we met that the likelihood of a romantic encounter would be negligible, but she was fun and I liked talking to her, so we met as two friends. After the first date, we kept in pretty close touch with each other. We talked on the phone about once a week. We got together for coffee and some fun every couple of weeks, and we were really good friends. There were a few occasions when we knew of some rock groups from Central Jersey playing, and we both got together with friends and had some really good times.

In a previous folder in this chapter, I described a date with a woman who was a college professor. The night of that horror, I immediately beeped Fran and said, "Fran I just had the date from hell." She called me right back on my cell phone and said, "Dennis, that's impossible! I just did. I must have been dating her brother!" We both made it to a local bar where we closed the place talking about how bad our dates were.

Fran and I became real confidants and she helped me understand a lot about dating. She was the one who told me, "Never, never take a date to dinner on the first date. Meet for coffee or just have a drink. If it works out, dinner is an excellent follow up date."

I knew going into the first date with her that we would be friends, and I was right. There was no expectation of anything more. That became an attitude that I would later adopt throughout my whole philosophy on dating. With no expectation, there can be no disappointment. Fran, even though she was a decade and a half younger, proved to have the advice I needed and I certainly thank her for it.

Now I talk to her every so often, but like some of the other Internet friends that I've made, she knows that if she ever needed me I would be there in a heart-beat. I feel just as confident that if I needed her, she would do the same. I wish there were more Fran's out there. The Internet would be a much better place.

Case Study Number Eleven
Name: Carol
Screen Name: CutterOne
Location: Long Island, NY

Carol responded to a personal ad that I ran. She seemed impressed right from the start, and although she was really at the outer limits of how far I'd like to travel, we e-mailed back and forth. There was no immediate spark here; it just went along slowly. In a matter of a few weeks, we eventually wound up making some chat dates and met each other online at a predetermined time. That got old fast, so we just exchanged phone numbers.

The phone talk was really comfortable. It seems for whatever reason, some people have a real natural phone personality. Our comfort zone was almost immediately established. Carol and I got into the habit of talking briefly about once a day, and about every third day we spent some quality time on the phone. There were a lot of things that we had in common, and we really liked finding things out about each other.

The course of our conversation took a turn to planning a date, and it was decided that we would go to the movies in Manhattan. We decided we would meet, see a movie and maybe get something to eat. All the plans were set. There was no overwhelming expectation. We saw each other's photos. The problem came when we met face to face. There was that chemistry thing again hitting both of us right on the heads. It just didn't happen.

There is no lesson here. It was just simply an example of how sometimes it works and sometimes it doesn't. You never know, however, until you try.

Case Study Number Twelve
Name: Donna
Screen Name: The Queen
Location: Jersey City NJ

Donna and I met by chance. She happened to be scanning the member's directory and she flagged me down. It was instant message back and forth for just a few minutes when we exchanged phone numbers. As it turned out, she wanted to ask me a legal question because she saw law enforcement in my members' profile.

Whenever someone instant messages me, the first thing that I do is look them up in the member's directory. I saw that she had in her own personal profile that she was a "celebrity". Well, she was a person of notoriety—that was for sure. As it turned out, she was in a movie as a guest, and the movie was really a bigger picture. It had national media coverage and was eventually shown on HBO.

Well, Donna had a web site and I was interested in working with her on the promotion of the book. She actually lived a half-hour away, and we decided to meet for a date. Well it wasn't love at first site, as a matter of fact there wasn't any chemistry, but we did become friends. Donna went on to other projects and she makes frequent radio appearances on New York radio.

The whole point of putting her story into my book is that you never really know who you are going to meet and what possibilities may come from keeping an open mind.

Case Study Number Thirteen
Name: Dori
Screen Name: NYGurl
Location: New York City

Dori responded to a personal ad that I had posted. She went overboard on her response, and it seemed that she really was attracted to everything that I wrote. We e-mailed each other for about a week when we finally caught up to each other on instant message. It only took a couple days before we exchanged phone numbers.

The phone conversation was really very comfortable. We talked a lot about each other, and we were really getting to know each other fairly intimately. She was in her late thirties, and she was not at all immature from every indication. She told me on every occasion that she saw my picture and that she liked it. In addition to that, she continued to tell me that looks were not an important factor to her, that personality was most important. So things moved along at what seemed to be a sensible and very comfortable pace.

We talked on the phone at that point every day, not entirely for long sessions, but just kept in touch with each other. She seemed like a caring person, and someone whom I felt very comfortable with. I thought that she might be a "keeper".

She also worked in the legal field, and we had some common ground there. She was responsible, and had a summerhouse at the shore. I was really beginning to think that there was at least some relationship potential here. Our relationship by phone was going on for about a week and a half, and we made a solid date. Things seemed like they were going to progress to a very nice comfort zone for us, and it seemed foolproof.

I drove over to New York and met her at her apartment. Once again, that is something that is almost never done. She showed me her apartment and gave me a great big hug and a kiss. This was really good. The date consisted of us going to her neighborhood bar, where she introduced me to some of her friends. We ate there and watched a ball game. We ended up at her apartment where we took about three hours getting to know each other better. She invited me to spend the next weekend with her at her shore home. Everything was set and things were looking good. The attraction was there. She had a nice apartment and things seemed quite normal. She was a very good kisser too!

I had talked to her on the phone the next day and we both were looking forward to the car trip to her shore home about four hours away. It was going to be a chance to really relax, get to know each other, and find out if this was something we might want to do more of. I had actually made an appointment in New York with a publisher for earlier in the day, and I was supposed to pick her up after that in the afternoon and go off to the shore for the weekend.

The day I was leaving for New York, I was all packed. Dori called and said, "I am so sorry about this." I thought she was canceling the trip because something happened! She went on to say, "Remember when we were talking about the chemistry thing?" I said, "Yes?" She went on "Well it's just not there!" This had taken me by surprise because it was the first time she even came close to mentioning anything like this. As it turned out, this whole relationship of great conversation, tremendous compatibility, some fairly good common interests (and the kissing wasn't bad either) just went bust!

In the final analysis, I had a sense that she had a few boyfriends or "irons in the fire", and she was doing a little bit of a juggling act. I kind of got to take a better look at things in retrospect and saw that the times when she did call were usually very early in the evening or much later. This would lend me to believe that she had been calling me just prior to or just after a date.

It's not unusual for men or women to juggle a few romantic interests, or to want to trade up for the best situation. I can say honestly that this late in the game I was a little surprised because I felt that I had actually been played. I cannot say for sure if this was the case. At the restaurant, Dori insisted that she pay for half the check, so she wasn't in it to take advantage of me. She may have just been looking for Mr. Perfect, something that I know very well.

It was surprising, though, the way the whole whirlwind romance went. The day she cancelled I was all packed and ready to go. I was annoyed at the short notice, and felt a little rejected. After a day or so, though, it was really all for the best. In this whole dating ritual, if you can get in and get to know the person fast and make a conscious and responsible decision quickly, it really saves everyone involved from getting too emotionally involved and experiencing the whole pain that comes from ending a relationship.

Dori was really very nice. I haven't heard from her since. Perhaps she did find Mr. Perfect, or perhaps she is still looking. Whatever the case may be, I had a great time with her while I did, and I wish her all the best.

Case Study Number Fourteen
Name: Ginger
Screen Name: HarlemGrl
Location: Middlesex County, NJ

I met Ginger quite by accident. We chatted for a while and eventually we exchanged phone numbers. She was the perfect example of a player. She was a little older than most women that I am used to dating. I had thought that she wanted the same things that I wanted, which were a relationship, a comfort zone and some good companionship. That wasn't the case. Having been recently separated, she had made it a habit of playing to my sympathetic nature. I wasn't aware of this until later after we parted ways. Once again, I know that I should have trusted my "gut" reaction to all of this and I should have even listened to my friends. There wasn't ANYONE who really had ANYTHING nice to say about her, but this was a perfect example of the expression, "love is blind".

She had formulated an entire fictitious life story about how she had never gotten anything from her husband and how she was really happy to be with a man who knew how to treat a woman right! Needless to say, she fed my ego, and I honestly liked the stroking that my ego received. There were a ton of warning signs that I consciously chose to ignore, among them an unbalanced nature and extremely erratic behavior.

She was extremely distraught over the treatment her husband had given her and she had a restraining order placed on him. She seemed very happy to be dating someone in law enforcement; it seemed to give her a sense of security. I dedicated my whole life to helping people just like her. It was natural for me to do my best to in some small way, to give her the solace that she needed. My friends did not agree and many people whom I am very close with said, "Stay away, she is trouble." But I didn't listen!

She latched onto me as a result of extreme acts of violence that her ex-husband had perpetrated upon her. She showed me all kinds of marks and scars on her body from closed fist punches and kicks, like when he kicked her down the stairs and physically prevented her from dialing 911. That was all it took for me—my protective nature kicked in immediately. I knew that this could be trouble, but she played me with a level of sincerity that just captured my heart. So over the course of several months I dated her and did my best to try, in some small way, to help eradicate the pain that she was carrying. It turned out in the end that all the sincerity was completely one-sided.

I had done for her, in the months that I was with her, more than her ex-husband had done in years, except for one thing. I would not be abusive to her.

Towards the end, as our relationship was falling apart, she tried every way possible to get me to become abusive. She took almost everything that we had done together and began a week long tirade of insults and petty criticisms against all of my efforts. It had become obvious to me that it wasn't her that was making these assessments. She finally admitted that she had been taking calls from her ex-husband all along, and that just recently the two of them had decided to work things out. He even talked her into dropping her restraining order against him.

So, once again, I learned a valuable lesson. Don't date people who are not at the same "level" as you, being that it takes time from separation to divorce. Also, don't date people who are self-destructive AND co-dependent.

Case Study Number Fifteen
Name: Marta
Screen Name: Marta1972
Location: North Jersey, NJ

Marta was a perfect example of what I would call a low-level player, or a player of opportunity. She was the perfect example of an opportunist. Moreover, she had a very interesting approach to the game, and she actually had a pretty good system of accomplishing what she wanted.

Marta had been scanning the member's directory under the above screen name for anyone having to do with law enforcement or law. She was looking for, and wanted as many contacts in either field that she could find. When she either e-mailed or instant messaged the "target", it was quite natural to do a quick scan of the member's directory and check out her profile.

Her profile had a very convincing combination of "all the right stuff". In it she had that she was a single female, twenty-five years old. Just the right age to begin a serious relationship with a man in his twenties or thirties. She had an educational background that said she had her bachelor's degree in criminal justice, and that she was in college, in search of a real job. In addition to that, what she wrote in the hobbies entry had probably everything that would make her a man's dream including: rollerblading, fishing, sports, country music, car races, sporting events. I'm actually surprised that she didn't have hunting or wet T-shirt contest winner. I guess she didn't want to appear too "down and dirty." Her marital status was SINGLE—what a surprise.

To understand my point, in case it escaped you, she was a guy-magnet! Everything in her profile indicated that she would be the girl involved in everything a man would want his mate to be involved in. She had, however, specifically and strategically targeted both the law and law enforcement field. As luck would have it, I took the bait when she e-mailed me, and we exchanged e-mails for quite a while. I later found out that she wasn't in any rush because she had actually been doing the same with about a dozen other police officers and about a half a dozen lawyers. I think she might have even had a judge in there somewhere.

It progressed naturally (again, surprise!) to an exchange of telephone numbers and again, following true to her methods, the calls continued for a few weeks before she agreed to meet. She was juggling a whole cadre of people who were somehow involved in law. I would think at this point one might think that she was "job hunting." That would make sense, and be a noble and honest reason for her efforts, except for the fact that she already had a job—she was a waitress. Need I also mention that everything else in her profile was a lie, and she just used it as bait? People who are already in a profession tend to try and help others who sincerely want to get into the field. It's a kind of mentoring. Many senior police officers often encourage their young proteges to take the police test and come into the job. Many lawyers and judges work with understudies who clerk and do other work to get a break in the business. Together, we often encourage these young neophytes to work their way in, and then work their way up.

So, it was natural to see from her profile, had it been sincere, that she was one of the many who would have liked her chance to make her mark in society by launching her way into public life. None of that was the case. I met her at a North Jersey restaurant, and we talked. I asked her several times about her interest in the law. She gave a very evasive response. Instead of actually engaging me in conversation, she was more interested in the "contacts" I had, and at the same time flirted with me. Her flirtations were very suggestive and she had it down pretty well for a junior level player.

It didn't take too long before I saw that she was just on a fishing expedition for information, and I got real serious, real fast. She got a little put off and maybe even a little afraid. So, she came clean and told me what her whole "deal" was. I learned at least half of it the first time we met, and then on a subsequent visit. I got her to tell me the total truth. I more or less told her that I wanted nothing to do with her if she continued to evade and lie, and that if I heard of anyone else that she had been in contact with, I would tell them her game.

Marta was just another young woman who found herself in a co-dependent, abusive relationship. She had gotten herself involved with a man who controlled her and everything about her. Her job, her time off and her life were all dependent upon his approval. She was an intelligent and very attractive young woman, but nonetheless, she could not break free from his control. She had been with him since she was seventeen years old. He had beaten her and abused her. She got a restraining order against him on several occasions, and had it lifted just as often. She was reaching out to whomever in the legal profession for free advice, for support or for any emergency contact she could have in case he hospitalized her.

I gave her information for several women's groups for legal services in her area, and for the appropriate law enforcement official that she could contact. I provided her with a package of information that would have given her a new lease on life. In the end, it turned out that all she was actually looking for were just other ways to keep her man from going to jail. She wanted any contact with law enforcement, lawyers or judges to help him to beat the system. She was actually "out there" working for him as an information prostitute. He was involved in other activities that caused him to cross paths with the law, and she would have done anything to keep him from going to jail.

The last time I checked, her profile had been updated slightly so that it would now attract even more men into her life, and when I spoke to her last, she was still trying to do her best to help him out. She had lost her waitressing job because he had come into the restaurant and started to beat her up. When I asked her about it, she said it really wasn't his fault and that she provoked him!

Case Study Number Sixteen
Name: LongIslndGrl
Screen Name: Karla
Location: Long Island, NY

The very, very brief online relationship with Karla that I had serves to illustrate one important point. If you are truly interested in having any kind of relationship AT ALL, you need to ask at least some questions and get a few answers.

Karla was not a player. Obviously, she was pretty new to Internet dating and the whole concept. She is not unique in that respect, and actually, she does serve as a good example of what not to do when striking up a friendship that you hope leads to something more.

She answered one of my personal ads and in the ad form, there were the usual questions about marital status, age, race, height, weight—all of the usual inquiries. This particular form, for whatever reason, didn't have a field about children. I am guessing it was either overlooked or they figured that you would put it in the narrative. I never volunteer any information that is too personal, I always figure those things can be answered on the phone. As it turned out, Karla never asked about kids and we began a great dialog through e-mail and eventually on the phone. We talked on the phone for over a week, and were in the process of setting up a date. I mentioned that it could not be *this* weekend because I had my kids. So we planned to meet the following weekend. That night I turned on my computer and had this really terse e-mail from her saying that she needed all the attention, and that she didn't know I had kids. She said she was sorry and that this could not work out. I tried to call her, but she didn't answer the phone and she would no longer respond to any of my e-mails.

The main lesson to be learned from that experience is that if you met someone in person, you would probably ask certain questions right off the bat. For example, "Are you married?" Do you have any children? Are you employed? I am suggesting that there is no harm in getting crucial questions right out of the way from the very start. It is certainly better to find out before you invest a lot of time and effort, only to have this very abrupt cut-off later on.

The other suggestion that I feel is very important is that if things are not what you expected or anticipated for some reason, part in an honest and sincere way. It is just plain bad Internet manners never to have contact again. As I indicated in an earlier part of this book, there are thousands of players coming into this game across the country each and every day. However, I also said that the people with whom you are in contact cross paths from time to time. There's nothing wrong with being honest, stating your position and leaving as a friend. If that is what you would do in the real world, why do anything less in the cyber-world?

Case Study Number Seventeen
Name: Lisa
Screen Name: DeFiance
Location: South Jersey

Lisa was a prime example of an experienced player. She was one of those people who was smooth, polished and had her whole system down. I have to admit this experienced female game master caught me off guard.

She responded to my personal ad and we went through a series of e-mails. Now here is a clue that you should really pay attention to: most players when they are "working" several people at once, don't really have the time, or aren't interested in investing the time it takes to establish a legitimate relationship. So while you are pouring out your guts to these people or writing them a story of your life that would rival *War and Peace,* they are coming back at you with pat, short, simple answers or dialog. That is usually an indicator that they have several fish on the hook, and they can't possibly write in detail to all of them.

As I have said so many times before, the clues are always there, and this case was no exception. For whatever reason, I didn't pick up on them. So we started this dialog by e-mail that eventually wound up as an exchange of phone numbers. On the phone it seemed (now in retrospect) to be more of the same. Just short conversation, almost as if blocks of time were being allotted. We did talk, however, and we were comparing notes back and forth as to how compatible we might be.

I wasn't all that excited about this relationship/friendship, so I wasn't making an emotional commitment. It was just going along at a steady pace, and I honestly did think that something would come of it.

By this time I had was experienced enough to know that sometimes things do go slowly, and sometimes things move along faster than expected. This happened to be a slower than usual movement, and it wasn't unique. What was actually missing, though, was a steady progression in time. Usually as two people get to know each other better, and, if they like each other, they will spend PROGRESSIVELY more time either in e-mail, chat or on the phone. In this case, I now realize that was the indicator. It was as if I was being, once again, allotted blocks of time instead of having a growing dialog that we both would have enjoyed.

I did begin to press for the face to face date so that things wouldn't continue to move along, and I'd have my expectations kicking in. Lisa seemed to want to put the date together also. Seemed is the operative word, because she didn't offer ANY ideas or plans, but was agreeing with many of my ideas. I had invested about six weeks, which is just about my ultimate limit for pen pals, phone buddies, chat friends—whatever you want to call them. After that point if there is no date, I am breaking off the relationship because I am aware at that time that the other person is playing, or they have no intention of actually meeting me.

I said to Lisa that this was the week that we should meet. She became very irate, and said that she thought the fact that we were of different religions was a problem. I must state here that although I am a Christian and she wasn't, this had NEVER been a problem and never came up in conversation at all.

We both knew there was a difference, because that was information that was prominent in the personal ad. It was something I had discussed during our first contact. I know that is a stickling point for some people, and I get all of that out of the way right up front.

As in the past, issues like children, past marriages, current marital status and religion should be talked about before anyone gets too involved. In this case, although I was a Christian and she wasn't, we both enjoyed the fact that we liked the whole "New Age philosophy." Much of our conversation had revolved around some of the artificial barriers people put up around themselves that tended to isolate them from what would be an otherwise wonderful relationship.

So we never met. She developed a rapid set of issues and injected them into several final conversations. My thoughts are that she was either married or she was playing several people at once. All along while doing that, she feeling them out to see who was the best "package."

That is not that unusual, and in fact also happens in the real world, not only cyber-space. The caution here, though, is that most people have difficulty lying to your face, and if it is happening in the real world, it usually can't go on all that long before you pick up on the signals. In the cyber-world, it is much easier to deceive a nameless, faceless person. They are or they seem to be a non-person, and the game is played out accordingly. For your benefit, however, I have shown you some of the clues that you can get from their behavior. If someone isn't placing the same amount of time or effort into getting to know you as you are, well, just take a step back and try and get a better look.

Case Study Number Eighteen
Name: Unkown
Screen Name: GIJoe
Location: Bosnia, Yugoslavia

This is not a story that I personally experienced, but one that was told to me recently, and it just exemplifies how pervasive this whole concept of Internet game playing actually is.

A friend of mine called, and was telling me that she had a friend who was a middle-aged woman who had met a "fine young man" on the Internet. Apparently the man was a marine, had a laptop and was communicating with her for quite awhile. After several weeks, this marine told her that he was being shipped off to Bosnia to take part in the military operations there. Of course, the woman had begun at least a friendship with this man, and she had concerns.

The two of them had exchanged telephone numbers, and although she could only e-mail him, he was able to occasionally call her. Months had gone by, and under the circumstances, they had not had the chance to meet. As things moved along, she was anticipating a great relationship, and he had given her every indication that he felt the same way. She was into her fifties and this marine apparently was in his thirties, but as life and love would have it a May—September romance seemed to be in the making.

Throughout the trials and tribulations of war they had apparently grown together, and without so much as a touch of a hand or a glimpse of an eye. He proposed to her from war torn Bosnia over the telephone and she accepted. Of course she e-mailed him every chance she had, and it looked like a true Internet love story.

She had some money that she had saved throughout her life, and she made all the arrangements for that fateful day when her man would come home. She completely redecorated her home professionally, and also refurbished it to what she thought would be his liking. Throughout the whole process, she probably spent a good portion of her life's savings to accommodate her long-distance lover.

Thousands of hours later spent on the computer, hundreds of e-mails and tens of thousands of dollars, all in preparation for her life to begin anew, were all focused on his arrival date. He had phoned her and had given her all the details of his arrival at Newark International Airport. She was there waiting with balloons and a limo. She waited and waited and waited. After the waiting, of course the worrying began. He never showed up. After days of frenzied attempts to find him, she finally was able to locate someone in his military company that told her he had shipped out back to his home in the Midwest.

The woman finally was able to track down a family member who told her that they were sorry for her, but he was now too "embarrassed" to talk to her. He had no intention of marrying her, and because of being lonely in the war zone, just got caught up in everything. It nearly destroyed the woman, and it was a cost that she would never be able to recover.

I guess all the lessons in this speak for themselves, but the same theme I have told you time and time and time again comes to mind. Please don't let your emotions rule your reason.

There are at least another hundred or so folders of case studies that I could have written into this book. The question is, when does it become repetitive, and how much is too much? I have shown you here by my experience as a police officer, by my many years in crisis counseling and behavioral science, that even after literally dozens upon dozens of dates I could be "played".

A Final File Note

One last amusing story comes to mind that I thought I should share with you. It just goes to show you that you never know who is on the other end of the electronic line that you might be pouring your guts out to.

It was in the early morning hours that I decided to "see" who was around, and I was actually going in and out of the chat rooms looking at what was happening. I was a little bit tired and about ready to log-off line. I wasn't all that excited about who was on and what was going on anyhow. Because I was tired, I was not really as sharp as I might normally be.

My instant message window popped up:

HOTSTUFF:	Hi!
DenisJrsey:	hi
HOTSTUFF:	busy?
DenisJrsey:	just about ready to log-off actually…
HOTSTUFF:	want to chat?
DenisJrsey:	sure

> *** So I go to the member's directory and thought I'd see who it was that I was chatting with…

Member Name:	*Chrissie*
Location:	*New Jersey*
Birthdate:	*11/12*
Sex: *Female*	
Marital Status:	*Single and Looking*
Hobbies:	*trying to find the right guy, hanging out with friends, reading, sex*
Computer:	*This one*
Personal Quote:	*Just do it!*
DenisJrsey:	so Chrissie, what are you doing up this late at night?

HOTSTUFF:	looking for guys
DenisJrsey:	and how did you find me?
HOTSTUFF:	member directory
DenisJrsey:	so have you found anyone else
HOTSTUFF:	all the time
Denisjrsey:	so where in Jersey are you

HOTSTUFF:	Edison
DenisJrsey:	that's cool I'm about ten minutes away.
HOTSTUFF:	that's real cool
DenisJrsey:	So do you have a pic?
HOTSTUFF:	Nah, never send em
DenisJrsey:	So what do you look like
HOTSTUFF:	I'm cute
DenisJrsey:	I see you don't type very much detail
HOTSTUFF:	what do you mean
DenisJrsey:	well....I'm trying to find out some things about you, you know the usual stuff, career, height, weight, age, all the critical stuff, I'm just wayyyyy too tired for small talk I figured I'd get right to the point
HOTSTUFF:	I go out with guys all the time, they like me
DenisJrsey:	well that's cool but maybe their standards are lower than mine ::::laughing::::
HOTSTUFF:	they all say I'm nice
DenisJrsey:	No Doubt! But I've been down THAT road before!!!!
HOTSTUFF:	what road, you don't know where I live

    *** Now I'm wondering, is she being cute, evasive or is she nuts!

DenisJrsey:	so tell me something about yourself
HOTSTUFF:	what do you want to know

    *** She is definitely being cute here, I re-read her directory profile, she was born November 12th.

DenisJrsey:	So you are a Scorpio huh, November 12th?
HOTSTUFF:	what do you mean
DenisJrsey:	Astrological sign, I'm a Capricorn and you?
HOTSTUFF:	I dont know about that stuff

    *** Now I re-check the members directory and I scroll up the chat log and notice she isn't using any capitalization or punctuation.... RED FLAGS!

DenisJrsey:	It would seem obvious that since you are such a worldly person, you would be able to discern a quality specimen of man when you encounter one in the midst of this electronic wonderland
HOTSTUFF:	what are you talkin about
DenisJrsey:	I am talking about YOU!

	*** It's way too early in the morning for this game playing stuff, and she just doesn't seem to be getting it.
HOTSTUFF:	I thought you would be fun to talk to
DenisJrsey:	yes, I am but I can't seem to get to know anything about you, that's why I asked if you are a Scorpio.
HOTSTUFF:	I dont know if I am
DenisJrsey:	Well isn't your birthday November 12th
HOTSTUFF:	no it is in june
DenisJrsey:	well why does it say November 12th in the member's directory
HOTSTUFF:	I dont have my birthday there
DenisJrsey:	yes you do
HOTSTUFF:	no I dont
DenisJrsey:	I just saw it
	*** it was way, way to late for this nonsense, and I was just about to pull the plug on this conversation, when it hit me like a ton of bricks!
DenisJrsey:	wait a minute! How OLD are you
HOTSTUFF:	i am 11 and i will be 12
DenisJrsey:	GOODNIGHT CHRISSIE!

The online players, as I said before, come in all shapes, sizes, colors, and ages. It never even dawned on me that this little pre-teen was playing around. I was caught off guard and not thinking when I saw birthday in the member's directory I just naturally thought it was just that, her BIRTHDAY!

I am sure that I'm not the first person to make that mistake, nor will I be the last. But if she started making some suggestive small talk, I could have easily wound up in trouble. I have heard a lot of stories that were very similar to mine, and that gives me cause to wonder where all of this is going. I am happy to have been able to share these experiences with you, and I hope that in the process you have gained some valuable insight. The players come disguised in many different forms. They could easily be seen for who they are...but we fail to take notice. We allow our hearts—being poor substitutes for our brains—to make these very critical decisions.

At the end of it all, I am sure that I will make a few more mistakes myself, always looking for the good in another person. I'd like to think that I have finally found that one very special, truthful and genuine counterpart of myself. I am also sure that you too will make some mistakes along the way.

I would hope though, because of this effort on my part to share with you these trials and tribulations, *your* mistakes will be less crucial and *your* pain lessened because you are a little better prepared. Life is a chance; it is a game in and of itself. I hear my father's words echo in my ear many times when he would say, "you can go outside and get hit by lightning." Of course that's true. You never know what fate holds in store for you. But I know that as far as I am concerned, I'd like to have at least enough control in my own life to be responsible for the decisions that can hurt me or cause me irreparable damage.

I wish you all the best in your efforts to find friendship and true love on the Internet, in the personal ads or even down the street corner, or in the local mall. Everyone deserves the happiness that comes with true love. It is not all that elusive and everyone is not a game player. It just helps when you have a friend along to help you keep your head on straight and your heart pointed in the right direction. Perhaps, in some small way, by sharing myself with you in this book I can be that friend.

Conclusion

122As this book draws to a close, I would hope that you recognize that I have bared my heart and soul here. Most of all, I would hope that you learned something. I claim ownership of this product. It was for me, a labor of love. I had some incredible personal tragedy. I would like to think that some of the Internet friendships I have made helped to get me through much of it. At times late at night, when I was alone with no one around and no ambition to go out, my online friends were like a Godsend. This book has become my confession and my reconciliation. For women, I would think that this would be a pillow talk book. For men, it would be a warning. This is a book about our "tribe." It's about the subculture that dwells in the bowels of cyber-space. It is a subculture that we seemed to voluntarily join, but inevitably found ourselves drafted into. Due to the behavior, we adopted to survive, a behavior we would not have chosen if choices were given.

Our tribe of emotional cannibals has turned us into an all-consuming electronically generated society of non-persons, living in cyber-space, playing cerebral games in electronic media that affect the all-too human hearts of all the players involved. This book was written to and for those players. The players who know who they are, but more importantly, the ones that don't even know that they are in the game!

The ending of this story is simple enough. I still have not found the perfect one. I know she is out there. I know, because she does exist in my mind. One day I'll meet her and know it. One day she may be right there in front of me, a few steps away. It might be that I have to answer another thousand or so e-mails, or she may quite possibly jump onto my screen as an instant message. I know though that one day I'll turn on my computer, and when everything is right and my number comes up, she'll be there waiting for me. She'll start out with Honesty, Loyalty and Friendship…

Epilogue

On October 1st, 1999, I placed a personal ad at Match.Com. I was a member there about a year prior, and met some very nice people. It is one of the best and least expensive of the computer dating services. They offer a seven-day free trial, which I encourage everyone to take advantage of.

They offer a wide range of personal selections and for the $11.95 per month that you pay, they have the best quality of people that I've found.

I received a reply to the ad that I posted from "Diane" on October 2nd, just a day after placing my ad. She seemed very nice, and she lived just one town over, about twenty minutes from my house. I wrote her back and she also had an AOL account. As luck would have it (and sometimes the hand of fate plays into our lives in the most unexpected ways) that afternoon (a Saturday) she was online. It turns out that she had also just joined Match.Com that same day. We chatted for a very short time and exchanged phone numbers.

I called Diane that afternoon, less than twenty-four hours after she posted her personal ad on Match.Com. Fate was at work here that day in Central New Jersey, and Diane broke all the traditional dating rules. After an hour or so of online instant messaging, she gave me her home phone number. After chatting on the phone for over an hour, she also agreed to meet me that same night. We both decided to meet at a large busy restaurant halfway between her home and mine. We were supposed to meet earlier in the evening, but something happened at my house and I had to push the date back about two hours.

It was no easy thing for Diane to get a babysitter on short notice, let alone get the babysitter, and then re-schedule her to come two hours later. It's difficult for single parents these days, and dating isn't something that can usually be done on a moment's notice. She was flexible, though, and that also impressed me. It seemed like she didn't have her feathers ruffled as easily as some women I had met in the past, and in the three or four phone calls we had that afternoon working out the details of our date, she was very amiable. These were all good things, and although I had a minor personal emergency going on at the time, we managed to laugh about it. I even arrived about twenty minutes late and still found her smiling. I got to the restaurant around eight p.m. that evening, and together we closed it after midnight. We spent another half-hour in the parking lot saying goodnight. We didn't want to seem all too anxious and, we even kidded with each other about that. We set our next date for Wednesday.

The next morning I turned on my computer to find an e-mail from her, saying that last night she lost her earring in the parking lot of the restaurant (sometimes that happens on long goodnights). I knew that by noon the lot would be filling up and the earring would be impossible to find. I took a ride there early that morning to see if I could find it. Fortunately, it was a bright sunny autumn day and there was no other car in the lot except mine. I started looking, walking back and forth and gazing at the ground looking for any glint of metal. I must have picked up a dozen or so pieces of glass, gum wrappers and other such trinkets but alas, no earring. I kept looking, after about half an hour I saw her car drive up with several small children in tow. Diane, her two children and her niece had just returned from church and were going to look for the earring. Well, it seemed we were on the same wavelength. We were there another ten minutes or so and there it was. I picked it up and she was delighted. I said as long as we were all there we might as well have brunch, and at this point the restaurant was just opening. Little did I know that my appearance there had a profound impact on her as an unprecedented act of chivalry (I found that out later).

Diane's kids and her niece were being typical kids, and she apologized for their behavior. Having two girls of my own the same age, it was just par for the course the way they were competing for attention and asking a hundred questions. It wasn't a romantic brunch with candles or anything at all like that, but it was very comfortable. Keeping to our pact, we re-affirmed our Wednesday date. We talked on the phone every day in between. Diane's father was a retired police Captain and we had a lot in common. She understood me better than most, and we really had some great laughs. In her personal ad she said that she wanted to laugh, and that all comes naturally to me.

On Wednesday I received a telephone call, and found out that a very close personal friend had been killed in an industrial accident. There was nothing more I could do after I visited with his family, so I found my way over to Diane's. She was very consoling and our date consisted of a quiet dinner and some unwinding. I had to be at the funeral for the next three days. During that time, she invited me over for dinner and attended the wake with me the last day. We were like two people who had known each other for years, and yet had only met a week prior. It was all so natural, and at the funeral she met most of my family. A month later, I had a family wedding and Diane came with me. We had a great time and everyone just adored her. It seemed that she had been everything I had been looking for. She fit right in with my family. Since that time, I've seen her just about every day or so. Our kids have met and we've done things together. We have both sensed that we feel like a family again. For both of us it's the first time in years. So, it looks like she's a keeper. I keep teasing her by kidding around, telling everyone we meet that we are *going steady*! We have now spent all the fall and winter holidays together. Thanksgiving, Christmas and New Years were so much fun together. It is sure nice not to be alone for the holidays. We talked about spending the four seasons together and maybe setting a date after that.

May 26th was the date we got married! It's been really nice with her; she actually edited this whole work. We work together and play together. We've celebrated together and experienced some tragedy together. Yup, she is a keeper. So it seems like it's really possible to find love out there, although Diane and I both agree that you have to kiss a lot of frogs.

And to think we did it all on the Internet! I guess the best way to finish this book is what I've been looking for all along, and what every good author always likes to read at the end of their work…

…and they lived happily ever after.

Dear readers,

Greetings from Cyberspace—I would like to thank you for reading Dating 911, The Ultimate Guide to Internet Dating Safety. I hope that it will help you in your quest for romance in today's uncertain world.

We'd love to hear from our readers about your internet dating success stories.

Our Dating 911 website is currently under construction (WWW.Dating-911.Com) and a Dating 911 workbook is in the works along with workshops that Diane and I plan to conduct to help others find happiness on the Internet.

On behalf of both of us, we wish you all success and romance in your quest for true love.

Dennis and Diane Nagy

The author can be contacted at Dating911@aol.com or through iUniverse.com

0-595-26333-X

www.ingramcontent.com/pod-product-compliance
Lightning Source LLC
Chambersburg PA
CBHW051247050326
40689CB00007B/1105